3/20

Nigel Slater's
TOAST

by Henry Filloux-Bennett

samuelfrench.co.uk

FOR AMATEUR PRODUCTION ENQUIRIES

UNITED KINGDOM AND WORLD
EXCLUDING NORTH AMERICA
plays@samuelfrench.co.uk
020 7255 4302/01

Each title is subject to availability from Samuel French,
depending upon country of performance.

THINKING ABOUT PERFORMING A SHOW?

There are thousands of plays and musicals available to perform from Samuel French right now, and applying for a licence is easier and more affordable than you might think

---

From classic plays to brand new musicals, from monologues to epic dramas, there are shows for everyone.

Plays and musicals are protected by copyright law so if you want to perform them, the first thing you'll need is a licence. This simple process helps support the playwright by ensuring they get paid for their work, and means that you'll have the documents you need to stage the show in public.

Not all our shows are available to perform all the time, so it's important to check and apply for a licence before you start rehearsals or commit to doing the show.

LEARN MORE & FIND THOUSANDS OF SHOWS

Browse our full range of plays and musicals and find out more about how to license a show
www.samuelfrench.co.uk/perform

Talk to the friendly experts in our Licensing team for advice on choosing a show, and help with licensing
plays@samuelfrench.co.uk   020 7387 9373

Acting Editions

BORN TO PERFORM

Playscripts designed from the ground up to work the way you do in rehearsal, performance and study

---

Larger, clearer text for easier reading

Wider margins for notes

Performance features such as character and props lists, sound and lighting cues, and more

---

+ CHOOSE A SIZE AND STYLE TO SUIT YOU

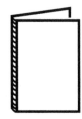

STANDARD EDITION

Our regular paperback book at our regular size

SPIRAL-BOUND EDITION

The same size as the Standard Edition, but with a sturdy, easy-to-fold, easy-to-hold spiral-bound spine

LARGE EDITION

A4 size and spiral bound, with larger text and a blank page for notes opposite every page of text. Perfect for technical and directing use

LEARN MORE | **samuelfrench.co.uk/actingeditions**

MUSIC USE NOTE

Licensees are solely responsible for obtaining formal written permission from copyright owners to use copyrighted music in the performance of this play and are strongly cautioned to do so. If no such permission is obtained by the licensee, then the licensee must use only original music that the licensee owns and controls. Licensees are solely responsible and liable for all music clearances and shall indemnify the copyright owners of the play(s) and their licensing agent, Samuel French, against any costs, expenses, losses and liabilities arising from the use of music by licensees. Please contact the appropriate music licensing authority in your territory for the rights to any incidental music.

IMPORTANT BILLING AND CREDIT REQUIREMENTS

If you have obtained performance rights to this title, please refer to your licensing agreement for important billing and credit requirements.

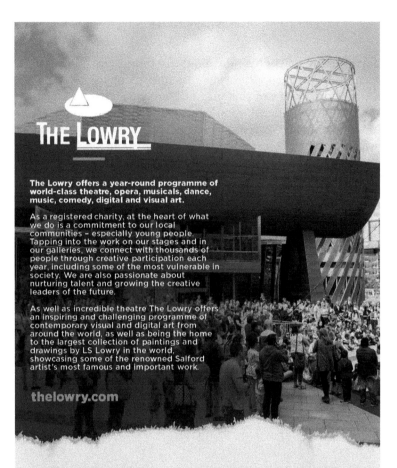

THE LOWRY

The Lowry offers a year-round programme of world-class theatre, opera, musicals, dance, music, comedy, digital and visual art.

As a registered charity, at the heart of what we do is a commitment to our local communities – especially young people. Tapping into the work on our stages and in our galleries, we connect with thousands of people through creative participation each year, including some of the most vulnerable in society. We are also passionate about nurturing talent and growing the creative leaders of the future.

As well as incredible theatre The Lowry offers an inspiring and challenging programme of contemporary visual and digital art from around the world, as well as being the home to the largest collection of paintings and drawings by LS Lowry in the world, showcasing some of the renowned Salford artist's most famous and important work.

thelowry.com

WEEK 53

In 2016 The Lowry launched Week 53; a bi-annual cross-arts festival of innovative, provocative, national and international work presented in a series of spaces including areas of The Lowry normally off-limits to the public.

Week 53 represents a major commissioning project for The Lowry – bringing together contemporary dance, visual arts, music and theatre in interactive installations, exhibitions and performances. Each festival we present and commission a week of themed programming that seeks to reward the compulsively curious, challenge convention and celebrate creativity.

 THE LOWRY ARTS COUNCIL ENGLAND Salford City Council

THELOWRY.COM/WEEK53

ABOUT THE AUTHOR

The author of a collection of bestselling books and presenter of nine BBC television series, Nigel Slater has also been the food columnist for *The Observer* for twenty-five years. His books include the classics *Appetite*, the two-volume *Tender* and *The Kitchen Diaries* trilogy. His memoir *Toast - the Story of a Boy's Hunger* won six major awards, has been translated into five languages and became a BBC film starring Helena Bonham Carter and Freddie Highmore. *Eating for England*, his collection of essays about Britain at the table, has been dramatised for BBC Radio 4. Nigel's 2013 book, *Eat*, won the National Book Award. Nigel has written a much-loved weekly cookery column, a sort of kitchen confessional, for *The Observer*, the world's oldest newspaper, since 1993. It is his curiosity and fascination for the details, and his observations of the small, human moments of cooking and eating that are the hallmark of his writing. Author, columnist, diarist and programme maker, Nigel remains very much an amateur cook. He is not a professional chef. His food is understated, handcrafted home cooking. He believes there is something quietly civilizing about sharing a meal with other people. "The simple act of making someone something to eat, even a bowl of soup or a loaf of bread, has a many-layered meaning. It suggests an act of protection and caring, of generosity and intimacy. It is in itself a sign of respect."

Nigel's writing has won the National Book Awards, the Glenfiddich Trophy, the James Beard Award, the British Biography of the Year and the André Simon Memorial Prize. Television awards include a Guild of Food Writers' Award for his BBC ONE series *Simple Suppers* and the BBC Food Personality of the Year. He is an honorary Master of Letters (MLitt). His most recent book, *The Christmas Chronicles*, was awarded the 2018 Fortnum & Mason Food and Drink Award for Best Food Book.

ABOUT THE WRITER

Henry Filloux-Bennett has worked for organisations including The Lowry, Bill Kenwright Ltd, Theatre Royal Haymarket, the Royal Shakespeare Company, Nottingham Playhouse and HighTide Festival. From 2010 to 2012 he was Artistic Director of the Old Red Lion Theatre in London, during which time the theatre enjoyed one West End transfer and one transfer off-Broadway. As a director and independent producer West End credits to date include Oscar Wilde's *The Importance of Being Earnest* (Theatre Royal Haymarket) and *Well* by Lisa Kron (Apollo Theatre). This is the third play he has written.

PRODUCTION NOTES

The play is set between the mid-1960s and mid-1970s and this should be apparent the audience, at least in the sound design, although how much further the production is rooted in the period past the sound is a decision for the creative team and company.

Staging should be bold, physical and fluid – there should be no need for blackouts / scene changes. Settings may be indicated and these worlds should be created with an approach that is light and playful. A world should be created where we think nothing of moving seamlessly and immediately between different settings. Stage directions are given with a purposeful lightness of touch – this is to allow maximum freedom to members of the creative team and company.

The only casting requirement is that the character of NIGEL should not be portrayed by a child or young adult; the actor playing him should also not play more than one part – he is the central point around which the story unfolds. The rest of the characters in the play can be played by as many or as few actors as desired, but the minimum to do the production justice would be a company of five.

As much as is possible the audience should be included in the play. At appropriate moments within the play, where the characters are eating something, it would also be lovely if the audience were able to taste or smell it too.

At the end of lines ' – ' indicates either a cue to be particularly tightly picked up, or an interruption.

FIRST PERFORMANCE INFO

Nigel Slater's *Toast* was first presented as part of The Lowry's
Week 53 Festival from 23 May to 2 June 2018.

Original Cast

Nigel – Sam Newton
Mum – Lizzie Muncey
Dad – Stephen Ventura
Joan – Marie Lawrence
Josh/Stuart – Andy Brady

Original Creative Team

Director – Jonnie Riordan
Designer – Libby Watson
Food Director – James Thompson
Sound Designer and Composer – Alexandra Faye Braithwaite
Lighting Designer – Andy Purves
Dramaturg – Ben Richards
Producer – Matthew Eames for The Lowry
General Manager – Rachel Candler
Production Manager – Ben Karakashian

For Gran.

CHARACTERS

MUM

NIGEL

FANNY

DAD

JOSH

WAITRESS

FLINCH 1

FLINCH 2

WARREL

MINNIE

AUNT ELVIE

UNCLE LEN

MRS E.

JOAN

AD 1

AD 2

MICHAEL

TRACEY

MISS A

ARNOLD

ROSE

DOREEN

STUART

LECTURER

SAVOY CHEF

ACT ONE

We start the play at home in Wolverhampton. Lights up on MUM *preparing for an afternoon's baking – she is getting ingredients out and sorting through various utensils.* NIGEL *is on his own, reading a cookbook.*

NIGEL *(showing the audience)* 'Cookery...in Colour'. By Marguerite Patten. The one and only real cookbook in the house. It's kept in the library. 'Library' may be a grand word. It's actually three Reader's Digests on a bookcase keeping company with some National Geographics, Dad's Dimple Haig, the Christmas maraschinos, and this...the cookbook. *(Reading from the book)* "A really up-to-the-minute cookery encyclopaedia, it contains not only interesting familiar recipes but also many very unusual dishes and a host of new ideas for meals of all kinds – *(looking through)* devilled kidneys. Spanish chicken. *(Finding a section in the book)* Duck! Mum? Is duck poultry? Or is it game?

MUM *ignores* NIGEL *and carries on her preparations.*

Mum?

MUM Nigel.

NIGEL Duck. Is it poultry? Or game? Only it looks like it could be either, and it makes a difference how you cook it! *(Reading)* "Poultry should not be overcooked. It not only spoils the flavour, but makes the flesh extremely difficult to carve" – look... *(Showing* MOTHER*)* Duck with orange sauce with port wine.

MUM Duck a l'orange.

NIGEL What's that?

MUM *That!* That's what they call it in fancy restaurants.

NIGEL Duck a l'orange. *(Reading)* "Peel two oranges and cut the peel into very narrow ribbons... Simmer in a little water... Meanwhile make a brown sauce with stock from the *giblets*"? – sounds disgusting! – add a little port wine, the orange strips and some of the orange stock. If desired add a little extra..." – Have you had it before?

MUM I can't imagine anybody actually cooks like that at home, Nigel – it's all very fancy. Now come and help me with—

NIGEL *(flipping to another page in the cookbook and still reading)* "Celebratory Desserts!" ...Shall we make a *(struggling)* crème... crème caramel?

MUM – Nigel, for goodness sake, come and help would you?

NIGEL *goes over to* **MUM**.

I've got everything together, we just need to measure it out.

NIGEL *(surveying the ingredients)* Six ounces of flour. Two ounces of butter. And our secret ingredient – one ounce of lard. That's according to Mrs Patten, anyway. According to Mum, it's—

MUM *(very roughly 'measuring' the ingredients in to the bowl)* Right. Bit more. There we go, that looks about right doesn't it.

NIGEL Mum doesn't stick to recipes.

MUM I do! More or less.

NIGEL More or less. Mum's answer to weighing out almost any ingredients for anything she's making.

MUM The cheek! Anyway, recipes are just someone else telling you what *they* like. These are *our* jam tarts, aren't they?

NIGEL Yes Mother.

MUM There we are then. So we make them the way we like them.

NIGEL It is five o'clock on a late summer afternoon and I am making jam tarts with my mum. Mum doesn't like cooking any more than she likes recipes. She does this for me. Every few weeks, out will come the big, cream mixing bowl, the rusty cookie cutters, the wooden rolling pin and... *(NIGEL breaks in to a big wide smile – he is in his element)* It's our little secret.

MUM Right then, over to you.

NIGEL Over to me. *(MUM goes to get a jug of water – NIGEL starts rubbing the ingredients together)* I start to rub it all together – tips of fingers, that's the key—

MUM – Higher.

> **NIGEL** *brings his fingers up.*

Bit more?

> **NIGEL** *raises his fingers higher as he mixes the ingredients together.*

Good. The higher up you do it—

NIGEL – The lighter it is. That's what Mum says, anyway—

MUM – It's *true*!

NIGEL And then Mum pours in a little cold water...careful Mum, not too much—

MUM – I know what I'm doing, thank you Nigel.

NIGEL She doesn't!

MUM Nigel!

NIGEL Just a drop more please, Mother! I bring the dough together in to a ball, and then it's back over to my mum, who gets to work flattening it out, ready to cut. She has small hands, but long, delicate, gentle fingers, and they roll back and forth over the pin. Why is it cracking?

MUM It's OK, we just pinch it back together. Like that, you see? Right, what filling shall we put in them?

NIGEL She asks me this every time. She knows the answer – there are only three kinds of filling that are allowed in a jam tart. Strawberry. Blackcurrant. And...lemon curd. I spoon just enough in to the centre—

MUM Not too much, we don't want them to boil over and stick to the tin do we?—

NIGEL – *but* still enough so there's more jam than pastry...and they're finished. Ready for the oven. They'll sit in the top bit of the Aga until they're done. Until the pastry's gone a pale sort of beige and the jam has just started bubbling around the edges. And while we wait...

MUM Toast?

MUM goes to make toast for them both.

NIGEL *(smiles brightly)* It's impossible not to love someone who makes you toast. People's failings, even major ones – like pouring too much water in to the jam tart mix – disappear as you break through the toasted crust and get to the doughy cushion of white bread underneath. It can be thick or thin, crisp or soft, gold or brown or black, or a bit of all three – but, like bed sheets and underpants, the perfect piece of toast can only ever be white. Mum says brown-bread toast is for old people – old people who suddenly decide they should look after themselves a bit more—

MUM – Damn it!

NIGEL Burnt. Mum burns the toast as surely as the sun rises each morning. In fact, I doubt if she has ever made a round of toast in her life that hasn't completely filled the kitchen with smoke. I am nine now and have never seen butter without black bits in it. But that's not the point...

MUM comes back, kisses NIGEL on the forehead and places the toast in front of him.

That's not the point at all. It is *impossible* not to love someone who makes you toast. *(Biting in to it, beaming, but then concerned)* – what's the matter?

MUM is having difficulty breathing – she goes over to get an inhaler from a drawer. She holds her hand to her chest and closes her eyes for a few seconds.

Mum?

MUM Nothing at all. The air's just a bit dry – now go and get yourself cleaned up and check on Auntie Fanny before your father arrives.

NIGEL Mum has asthma. Apparently she got it when she was expecting me – it's fine most of the time but sometimes, if the kitchen gets too hot, she needs a few deep puffs to make her feel better again—

MUM Did you hear me?

NIGEL I was explaining about your asthma—

MUM *Now*, Nigel.

NIGEL Like I was saying, it's *almost* impossible not to love someone who makes you toast. Right, come on, you'd better meet Auntie Fanny before Dad gets back. She needs to be checked on because she...pees herself...a lot.

FANNY sits in a chair, staring out and humming to herself. NIGEL waits.

She also sits...a lot. And smiles. And nods. Afternoon Auntie Fanny.

No response.

(louder) Afternoon Auntie Fanny.

FANNY looks up at NIGEL, smiles.

She keeps a tin of lemon bonbons with her at all times, but that's just a cover.

From somewhere appears a packet of Parma Violets. She hands them out to NIGEL, *tapping her nose – their little secret. He takes one out of the pack to eat, and offers one to* FANNY. *She taps her lemon bonbons and goes back to staring and humming.*

Sometimes I come and sit with her. She can't really hear much, and she smells. But I like her. And she's got a never-ending supply of these. She's not going to be playing a big part in the play. *(Pause)* To be honest this is pretty much it.

FANNY Speak for yourself.

NIGEL *(raising his voice)* We've just made jam tarts Auntie Fanny. Would you like one when they're done?

Pause.

FANNY No.

NIGEL *(carrying on regardless)* Mum might say she makes the jam tarts for me, but they're just as much for Dad – he loves them. Dad owns a factory that makes parts for cars. *Rover* cars. It's a bit of a drive away and it smells of oil, mostly. Dad doesn't though – he smells of Sweet Briar pipe tobacco. Oh, and greenhouse. I like smells. Well, you know what I mean – not *all* smells *(signalling* FANNY*)* – but still. I keep a list. *(Taking out a notebook)* I also like lists – I have a book of lists. Maybe just before she goes... *(To* FANNY *– raising his voice)* Auntie Fanny... I was just saying, just before you go—

FANNY – I'm not going anywhere thank you very much.

NIGEL OK. Well, just to make your part a bit more interesting then *(whispering to the audience) and* just before she goes, would you like to read out my list of favourite smells?

Pause.

FANNY No.

FANNY *continues to hum to herself. Pause.*

NIGEL Suit yourself. I'm sure she can hear better than she lets on – I think she just likes being different—

FANNY I'll have those off you if you're not careful.

NIGEL See what I mean? Right. *(Reading)* A list of Nigel's favourite smells, by Nigel Slater. Flapjacks. Old books. Snow. Roast chicken. Moss. The cress seeds sprouting on the blotting paper at school for our biology project. Jam tarts. Mum.

MUM *(taking the jam tarts out of the oven)* Yes?

NIGEL No, nothing. You were just being part of my list. Dad must love the smell of jam tarts too because *just* as they're coming out, in he walks.

Enter DAD.

DAD Good evening. *(He kisses* MUM, *gives her a box of chocolates)* I've eaten all of the soft nougat I'm afraid. *(He ruffles* NIGEL*'s hair, glances at* FANNY*)* Do you know what I saw coming up from town – *(Spotting the jam tarts)* Ohhh, jam tarts.

MUM What was that?

As MUM *is asking, he goes over to the tarts, takes one.*

DAD *(putting the tart in his mouth whole, not realising it's just come out of the oven, burning his mouth)* Coming out of Batkins, a white woman with a — *(He dances on the spot, hands flapping, trying to swallow. A flicker of a smile on* NIGEL, MUM *and* FANNY*'s faces)* Bugger it.

NIGEL So this is us. Me, Mum, Dad—

MUM – Go and have a drink of water for goodness sake—

NIGEL – and Auntie Fanny. And this is our house. Our three-apple-trees-in-the-back-garden, wood-panelled, downstairs loo, bluebells-along-the-path, cork-tiled world. We live in the Tudor-styled York House on Sandringham Road with a new bright red Queen Elizabeth post box just across the

street, and just up Victoria Street is the statue of Prince
Albert in Queen Square. Welcome to Royal Wolverhampton.

DAD   Or this evening, should we say *Roman* Wolverhampton!

NIGEL   I'm not sure that really works Dad.

DAD   – That's quite enough from you Nigel.

MUM   You're recovered then? Maybe that'll teach you to keep
your views to yourself.

DAD   And enough from you too, thank you. Right, come on. Are
we ready for our continental culinary adventure?

NIGEL   Tonight...spaghetti.

FANNY   A-what-y?

MUM   *(raising her voice) Spaghetti.* We're going to try it. Don't
worry, you don't have to eat it if you don't like it.

DAD   Right, Nigel, pan of water on to boil please. And this—

NIGEL   – *This* is a saucepan of reddy-brown stuff, bubbling,
like mini eruptions every few seconds—

DAD   – This is what we put on the pasta. Spaghetti Bolognese.

NIGEL   We've never had it before. Well definitely not me. By the
sounds of things Auntie Fanny hasn't, and from the looks
of things nor has Dad. Mum?

MUM   No, me neither. *(Picking up a paper packet of spaghetti)*
Tony, what do you do with these?

DAD   *(taking the packet from* MUM*)* These – go in here.

MUM   They're never all going to fit in there—

NIGEL   – He tries to read the instructions on the packet, but—

DAD   – Kathleen, my glasses?—

NIGEL   – he can't see. Mum hands him his glasses but they're
no use, because the instructions are—

DAD   – they're all in Italian?

FANNY I'm not eating that!

DAD You bloody well are! Maybe if we—

  DAD *starts breaking the spaghetti strands in to the pan.*

MUM – Be careful Tony, they're going all over the Aga.

NIGEL I watch and wait in silence hoping just maybe Dad will abandon the whole idea and let Mum make us some chops.

DAD I think it must be done by now—

NIGEL – Dad says after twenty minutes of boiling the spaghetti strands. He pours the contents of the pan in to the colander—

DAD – Plates, Kathleen. *(Beat)* Hurry up, they're getting away!

NIGEL We sit at the table with our plates, piled with pale yellow worms—

FANNY – I don't think I can.

DAD Hang on, wait for the sauce.

  He brings over the sauce and spoons it on.

MUM This looks very sophisticated. And it smells delicious.

FANNY It smells foreign.

DAD Just try it. *(He goes to get something)*

FANNY I don't even know how I'm supposed to eat it.

MUM Look – give me your fork. Here. Twirl it, you see? Like this.

FANNY He's trying to poison me.

MUM He's not. No, come on, *twirl* it. It's going all down your chin.

NIGEL Auntie Fanny's not a fan, but I quite like it. It's hot, salty, tomato-y, Bovril-y – not bad at all.

  DAD *returns with a drum of dried, grated parmesan.*

MUM What's that?

DAD I got it from Salt's.

NIGEL Percy Salt's is the grocer's on Penn Road, just down the hill. It's really two shops – the butcher's on the right and the grocer's on the left. Mum does most of her shopping there – between Salt's and Beatties in town there's not much you can't find. We'll go back there in a bit—

DAD – He said you sprinkle it on top. It's grated cheese.

DAD sprinkles it on his plate, and then offers it to FANNY.

FANNY Get it away from me, it smells of sick.

DAD offers it to MUM.

MUM I think I'm actually OK for now.

DAD lastly offers it to NIGEL, who sprinkles it on his food too. NIGEL stops, fork in mid-air, horrified, and puts the fork back down on the plate.

NIGEL *(whispering)* Dad.

DAD What?

NIGEL It does – it smells of sick.

DAD I know. Don't eat it. It must be off.

NIGEL We never have spaghetti bolognese, or parmesan cheese, again.

DAD This was a disaster.

Awkward silence.

FANNY How about something less *continental* for pudding?

DAD slams his cutlery down on the plate, gets up from the table and walks out, furious. Pause.

NIGEL He's gone to the greenhouse. It's his favourite place in the world, and in there with his tomato plants and flower cuttings and no spaghetti, everything's a bit better.

When I say plants and flowers of course I mean 'Antirrhinum' and 'Muscari'. Anyone? No? Snapdragon and grape hyacinth actually. Dad likes it when I call them by their proper old names – Josh has been teaching me them. Everyone meet Josh.

JOSH *the gardener enters with some gardening tools and a tin box containing some sandwiches. We are transported in to the garden.*

NIGEL Josh is our gardener. He does everything in the garden apart from mowing the lawn. Like carving the turkey at Christmas, that's Dad's job. Our garden is big. It's not *massive*, but it's big. There's a big apple tree in one corner which isn't ours but it hangs over our garden and if you stand on your tiptoes you can just about reach the apples. Dad's gardeners don't usually last for long – the last one let frost get on the dahlias and was gone within two weeks. But Josh is different. Dad likes him because he knows the proper names, and Mum likes him because she says he's as bright as a button—

MUM – and such a good-looking young man! –

NIGEL Mother!

MUM Sorry darling.

NIGEL I like him too. *(Pause – slightly embarrassed)* Josh has a motorbike, a black Triumph 250cc—

JOSH – it's a 3TA, 350cc, although I'm hoping to get a Speed Twin next year.

NIGEL So he's got that. And he brings his lunch in a tin box held together with an elastic band. He always has sandwiches, an apple and some biscuits – sometimes he gives them to me—

JOSH – Caramel wafer, or Bourbon?

NIGEL Ummm...

MUM *(appearing with a plate covered with a tea towel)* – Or flapjack?

NIGEL Mum!

MUM What?

JOSH *(taking one)* Thanks Mrs Slater.

MUM It's a pleasure Josh. Nigel?

NIGEL *(slightly embarrassed)* Thanks Mum. Flapjacks are usually a winter thing for my mum. They're one of the few things Mum makes – one of the few things Mum *can* make, and I love them. The chewiness. The sweetness and saltiness all at onceness. It's odd, Mum has been making a lot of flapjacks since Josh arrived.

MUM *(leaving)* Well then. I'll leave you two to it. Have fun.

JOSH Thanks again Mrs S.

NIGEL We both eat our flapjacks, and then he makes tiny little roll-ups while he sits on his bike, and—

JOSH – Right, let's be having you –

NIGEL – he lets me help, which none of the other gardeners have ever done.

JOSH Do you want to do the weeding in the front or the compost?

NIGEL *(considering)* Compost please.

JOSH Right, come on then. And after that we see how your corner is doing.

NIGEL My corner is my bit of the garden. Dad gave it to me last year and I'm allowed to plant whatever I want in it. For my first year I did cosmos, daisies and marigolds –

JOSH Nigel—

NIGEL Yes, sorry. Before my corner, the compost. I turn it with a giant, long-handled, two pronged fork while he works on the borders. *(Conspiratorially, he knows he should be concentrating on the task at hand)* This year I'm growing radishes. Josh is going to help me. Josh?

JOSH Oh, come on then.

JOSH *hoists* NIGEL *up on his shoulders and they charge around the garden playing aeroplanes until they crash in to the ground.* JOSH *takes out a packet of seeds.*

Open up your hands.

NIGEL *opens up his hands, and* JOSH *takes a packet of seeds, opens it, and pours some out in to* NIGEL's *cupped hands.*

Now, scatter them in to the lines in the soil.

NIGEL *starts to scatter the seeds.*

NIGEL They're such tiny seeds and they drop in little heaps in to the earth—

JOSH Be careful, not too close together. And not too many seeds.

Enter MUM.

MUM Nigel—

NIGEL Mum, come and look—

MUM Very nice, Nigel. Now, come on, in you go and get ready for bed and I'll come and tuck you up in a little bit.

NIGEL My mum always tucks me up. I think it's a sort of substitute because she can't play games or go to the park, on account of her asthma, and she can't make cakes, or, well, much else. One thing she can't blame on the asthma is the chaos she can create in the kitchen when anything more complicated than jam tarts is on the menu. Cue Sunday lunch.

We are back in the kitchen – a hive of industry, or chaos.

Pans are clanking and beef is crackling and steam is starting to fill the kitchen. Mum doing the beans –

MUM *takes a colander and pea pods over to* FANNY.

MUM Could you do the peas?

No response.

They just need – *(Speaking louder)* They just need shelling.

No response.

(going back over, giving up) Nigel, you do them instead then please.

NIGEL *goes over to collect the peas, smiling.* FANNY *winks.*

NIGEL Mum's doing the beans, *I'm* doing the peas, and Dad is safely in his greenhouse –

MUM *(shouting)* Tony! The Yorkshire!—

NIGEL – It's hot enough in here to melt lead – although to be fair most of the heat seems to be being given off by Mum. There are peas and carrots, potatoes, beef, gravy—

MUM – Oh God, the gravy!—

NIGEL – and then a huge Yorkshire Pudding—

MUM – *(shouting)* Tony!—

NIGEL – which Dad's in charge of, and which he makes in an old roasting tin and cuts into big podgy squares. That's all Dad has to do – he doesn't touch the gravy, though I think we all secretly wish he did. The best thing about Sunday lunch is pudding, which is always a boiled sponge. Whether it's raspberry, ginger, sultana or chocolate, I love each and every spoonful. We always have cream with it – Nestlé's from a tin – Mum couldn't cope with trying to make custard. Sometimes she forgets to top the pan up and lets it boil dry. Dad pretends not to mind but I can tell he's a bit annoyed that he's married a woman who can't even boil water –

MUM Nigel, would you mind if I made just a small point?

NIGEL Of course not, Mother.

MUM Well I just wanted to say that this whole exercise so far seems to be about embarrassing me in front of these lovely people. Perhaps it would be just a *little* fairer if you came up with a few examples for...*other* people.

FANNY Tony!

DAD – I'm warning you—

FANNY Tony!

MUM *(seeing the merit in* FANNY*'s idea)* Well—

DAD – Oh, she can perk up now –

FANNY *(remembering and laughing)* The percolator!

DAD – Will you shut up and suck a sweet or something?

NIGEL *(remembering as well)* The percolator! Oh yes, let's do that—

MUM – Well I don't know, it seems a little unfair doesn't it? –

DAD – Just you dare –

NIGEL We're doing it Father, I'm afraid. Right, places, come on both of you. Thank you Auntie Fanny.

It is a different afternoon – everyone helps to create the scene, although DAD *is less than impressed at having to take part in his humiliation.*

It's nearly four o'clock.

FANNY Excuse me young man.

NIGEL Yes?

FANNY It was my idea – so I'll do it, thank you very much – and you're not due back from school for a few more minutes. Right. There's a smell in the hall – part...burning rubber, and part...bitter. We open the door to the kitchen to see Tony with a shiny jug, which has been plugged in by the Aga, concentrating like his life depends on it. Tony. *(Pause)* –

NIGEL – Dad! Concentrating on it like his life depends on it.

He gives up and takes part.

FANNY Thank you. He's unusually red, tie crooked, and there's a...haunted look on his face.

MUM I'd say 'terrified'.

FANNY Let's say 'terrified' then. There's brown powder scattered all over the work top, and the metal pot is starting to make an odd sort of noise.

DAD – I think it's boiling the water –

FANNY – And enter young Nigel from school –

NIGEL – What *is* that?

MUM It's Dad's new coffee percolator –

FANNY I always wanted a perky copulator–

NIGEL I wonder what coffee tastes like, if I'm ever going to get to try it. I also wonder why Dad got the machine. He doesn't like coffee – I don't really know anyone who does –

MUM Let's have the china out shall we? And the coffee crystals.

FANNY Shortbread.

MUM All right but don't eat too many OK? Nigel could you put a couple petticoat tails on a plate for Fanny?

DAD Right, here we go.

He unplugs the pot and pours out the coffee. It hits the bottom of the cup, splashes straight back out in to the saucer and goes all over the table.

MUM For goodness sake, Tony, take the cup to the pot, you're making a right old mess –

DAD – The spout's too wide, it all comes out at once.

NIGEL And then silence. The verdict.

MUM Do you think maybe we put enough coffee in?

DAD I put exactly the right amount in.

MUM It's just it's a bit...

DAD What?

FANNY Watery? Thin? Pale? Burnt?

MUM No, it's –

NIGEL It's – *(Turning his nose up)* Interesting!

FANNY Why don't you put the kettle on Kathleen?

> *Beat.* FANNY *hands* NIGEL *a packet of Parma Violets as she goes to sit back down.* MUM *starts to put the china away while* DAD *disassembles the percolator, drying it and putting it back in the box.*

NIGEL Dad slips the instructions down the side as mum stands next to him with a look like of annoyance. That she's married a man who –

NIGEL – can't even boil water –

MUM – Thank you –

DAD – You can't compare this to boiling a pan of water dry!

FANNY It looks like we just *did* –

> The day after the day of the coffee percolator, I come home to find Mum ill.

> MUM *is sitting at the kitchen table, head bent down in her lap, eyes closed, breathing heavily and deeply. Socks in front of her, which she has been darning.*

> It's like she has to concentrate as much as possible to make her lungs work. Mum?

MUM *(struggling)* I'm fine, honestly.

> *She picks up a sock and tries to continue putting the thread through the needle, but can't quite manage.*

NIGEL Do you want me to do that?

MUM I'm not totally useless thank you. I've nearly done it now.

NIGEL You're ill.

MUM I'm not. I'm absolutely fine.

NIGEL Mum might be lying, but I'm actually *never* ill.

MUM That's not quite true, is it Nigel?

NIGEL Alright, but apart from the normal schoolboy illnesses –

MUM Measles –

FANNY – Stop scratching, you'll make it worse! –

MUM – mumps—

FANNY – Better to get it now than later on –

MUM – chickenpox—

FANNY – Don't pick them, they'll leave a scar! *(Giving him a packet of Parma Violets)* Here –

NIGEL – apart from them and a few colds and a tiny bit of flu, I'm very rarely ill. Aside from a mystery faintness, shivering and feeling sick which sometimes strikes around the time of —

DAD – Maths tests, football practice, the first day of term –

NIGEL – Thank you Father. It wouldn't be fair to say that I *enjoy* being ill. The sick bucket – sorry, you're eating *(if he can see an audience member eating a biscuit or cake or something)* – *(whispering)* sick bucket lurking not too far away. The thermometer being jammed too far underneath your tongue. And the worst part – tinned soup. Any normal parent might try something lovely like tomato. Not my mum. Cream of chicken. Cream of vegetable. Or in a spectacularly thoughtless moment – oxtail. Being ill *does* have a few things going for it though. Hot Ribena. Marmite soldiers. And jelly. To be honest it's worth the measles for a bowl of jelly on a tray every meal. Jelly's good even when Mum makes it, but the perfect jelly is – Aunty Fanny? How about this one?

He takes out his notebook and hands it to FANNY.

Look, this bit – it's about you.

FANNY   The Perfect Jelly, by Nigel Slater. Whether it be blackcurrant, orange, lime, raspberry – the flavour matters not. What counts is how loud the squelch is. Aunty Fanny's jelly is without doubt the loudest I've ever had. As a seasoned squelch sage she knows the key to making jelly that literally farts is to make it just a bit stronger than normal. Break the rules and use two packets of jelly instead of one for the same amount of boiling water. The measure of any jelly worth it's gelatine is its squelch.

DAD   *(entering, laden with suitcases and beach holiday paraphernalia)* – No time for squelching. Come on everyone. *(Pause)* Well, what are we waiting for? Here we go. Windbreak. Beach ball. Picnic basket. Bucket, spade, flags for the sandcastles—

MUM   Savlon?

DAD   Check.

MUM   Bite-eeze?

DAD   Check.

MUM   Plasters and cotton wool?

DAD   Check. And Dettol. And spare Ventolin for you. And... beach towels, and sun cream.

NIGEL   Everything needed for a Slater holiday. Oh, and a four hour drive.

FANNY   *Four* hours? Where are we going, Scotland?

DAD   Just get your things together and come on.

FANNY   Ohhh no, I am not going anywhere four hours away. Count me out.

DAD   Suit yourself.

MUM   OK well get everything else – you get the car out.

NIGEL   'Getting the car out' – a strange ritual in the Slater household consisting of my dad revving the car up for no apparent reason for about half an hour before we go anywhere.

DAD *sings* **"OH I DO LIKE TO BE BESIDE THE SEASIDE"**, *cajoling* MUM *and* NIGEL *in to joining in, despite their protests. We are transported to the seaside at Bournemouth.*

DAD Salt air, sunshine through the open roof in the car, seagulls squawking, and just over the hill, any second, beach as far as the eye can see...there we go – welcome to Bournemouth!

NIGEL Dad is it OK if I do the descriptions? It's sort of my thing.

DAD Your father can cope with a bit of amateur theatrics Nigel.

NIGEL Just concentrate on driving Dad. We head down to the front past all the big houses and the –

DAD Oh look, it's petunias this year –

NIGEL – Father, please! –

DAD – Sorry –

NIGEL – Thank you! We head down past the big houses and the neat formal flower beds, which, as Dad has already said, are petunias this year. This is our second year in—

MUM – There's a space! There. There!

DAD *(irritated)* – I can see it –

MUM – Well then –

NIGEL – Can I *please* do my –

MUM – Sorry, darling. You go ahead.

NIGEL This is our second year in Bournemouth and we're back in the same hotel and exactly the same spotlessly clean rooms as last time, the same breakfast – bacon and sausages for me and Mum, kippers for Dad. And toast. I love hotel toast. Cold and bendy in a little silver rack with even colder, rock-solid butter. The butter is nothing compared to the sea though, which is *freezing*. Mother insists on me wearing plastic sandals to go in, which are so tight, and the plastic so hard that they give me blisters. As if that's not bad enough Dad makes his annual attempt to get me in to ball games, which consists of kicking a ball at me, which hits me in the face with a shower of yet more sand. We have lunch at one of the open-air cafés along the beach. Just to carry on with the torture, Mum having seen battered fish and chips at the tables around us, asks the waitress for—

MUM – We'll all have chicken salad please.

NIGEL Why?! Who orders a chicken salad at the beach? When you can *see* battered fish the size of a beach ball right there?

MUM – And some bread and butter, please.

NIGEL – And why bread and butter? At home Mum is always buttering bread. I don't know why – no one ever seems to eat it.

WAITRESS No problem. Anything else? Any sauces? Salad cream? Maybe some ketchup—

MUM *(a touch too quickly)* Just the bread and butter will be fine, thank you.

NIGEL Did you see that? The *(recreates* MUM's *flinch)*? That's the Slater family reaction to ketchup. Tomato ketchup has never set foot in the house – I've only ever tried it a couple of times before. Dad will have mushroom ketchup with bacon, but never tomato ketchup. That *(recreates it again)* is also the reaction to a few other things. Take it away.

Enter FLINCH 1 *and* FLINCH 2.

FLINCH 1 Heinz.

NIGEL No idea why –

FLINCH 2 – It's a bit common. Crosse & Blackwell always better –

FLINCH 1 – Except salad cream of course –

FLINCH 2 – Absolutely.

FLINCH 1 French mustard.

FLINCH 2 Mustard just isn't mustard unless it's English.

FLINCH 1 Bien sur!

FLINCH 2 Typhoo—

FLINCH 1 – PG Tips—

FLINCH 2 – Taylors—

FLINCH 1 – Lipton—

FLINCH 2 – Tetley—

FLINCH 1 *Anything* that's not Twinings.

MUM AND DAD Twinings!

FLINCH 2 Camp Coffee.

FLINCH 1 Why *would* you when there's Maxwell House?

FLINCH 2 Margarine—

FLINCH 1 Awful –

NIGEL And lastly—

FLINCH 1 AND 2 HP Sauce –

MUM Wash your mouth out.

NIGEL And lunch is just the start of it. Dinner is a completely different story. Scrubbed clean, tie neatly tied, socks pulled up straight, it's a minefield –

DAD – Best behaviour, Nigel –

MUM – Comb your hair properly darling.

NIGEL Best behaviour is parent speak for remembering to say please and thank you just once too many times. Watch.

WAITRESS Good evening.

DAD Thank you.

WAITRESS Here are the menus –

MUM – Thank you.

WAITRESS I'll come back in a few minutes to take your order –

DAD Yes, thank you –

WAITRESS Can I get you some drinks in the meantime?

DAD Please, yes thank you – could we have a jug of water?

WAITRESS Of course.

DAD Thank you.

NIGEL See what I mean?

> **WAITRESS** *comes back with an iced jug of water.*

WAITRESS Here we go.

MUM AND DAD Thank you.

WAITRESS And anything special for you young man?

NIGEL Restaurant rule number one.

WAITRESS A list of Dad's rules for eating in a restaurant, by Nigel Slater. Rule number one. Do not ask for a drink – especially a fizzy one. Be happy with water –

NIGEL No thank you. I'm fine with water thank you very much.

WAITRESS – but...rule number two. Do not crunch the ice cubes in the water jug. Have you decided what you'd like then?

DAD Yes, please, we'll have steaks all round. Half portion for him.

MUM What does the steak come with please?

WAITRESS It comes with chips and peas.

MUM Lovely, thank you.

DAD Lovely.

WAITRESS Rule number three. Do not let your napkin slide on to the floor. Rule number four. Neither wolf down nor dawdle with your food. Five. Sit up straight. Number six. Do not under any circumstances wipe your mouth on your sleeve.

NIGEL After dinner we walk along the front. Mum seems fine again, and Dad is impressed with the flower displays along the way. Mum pulls her cardigan over her shoulders as a breeze comes off the sea, and as we turn to walk back to the hotel, I realise that life is pretty much perfect. I'm not sure if it's possible to be happier than I am at this moment.

We are back in Wolverhampton and JOSH *enters.*

But summer holidays can't last forever – especially when you've got radishes to harvest.

MUM Afternoon Josh.

JOSH Afternoon Mrs S.

NIGEL We're back at home, and it's the moment of truth.

JOSH Let's have a look, shall we?

NIGEL Josh gently pulls a set of leaves between his thumb and fingers, and –

JOSH – See? They're huge!

NIGEL At the end of the stem is a tiny pink radish, barely big enough to be recognisable.

JOSH Go on, try it.

NIGEL I do. It's crunchy. And hot. And mustardy. It's like my mouth's on fire!

JOSH They're great aren't they. Now, pick the rest of them and then we can give them to your mother.

NIGEL He gives me a little plastic bag and I put them in – about twenty of them – while Josh washes himself and gets changed back in to his motorbike bike leathers. I like it how he doesn't turn his back on me when he's drying himself—

Enter DAD.

DAD Nigel – *(Seeing* JOSH *– surprised and flustered)* What the bloody hell –

NIGEL – Look Dad, radishes.

DAD Go inside Nigel –

NIGEL – Would you like to try one?

DAD I said inside. Now. That's quite enough...gardening for one day.

Pause.

NIGEL The next week I come home his motorbike isn't there – instead there's an old man bending over the rose beds, with Josh's wheelbarrow at his side. *(Turning to* MUM*)* Mum? Where's –

WARREL *enters and knocks on the door.*

Mum?

MUM Josh won't be able to do the garden anymore.

NIGEL *Why?*

MUM That's enough Nigel.

WARREL *rings the doorbell again.* DAD *answers the door.*

WARREL Hello Mr Slater. Can Nige come out to play please?

DAD *(shouting)* Nigel! Friend here for you.

NIGEL Mum?

MUM I said *enough* Nigel. Go and play with Warrel.

NIGEL *(confused and angry with* MUM*, going over to* DAD *instead)* Dad, is it OK if I go and play with Warrel?

DAD Yes, but back for five, OK?

NIGEL Thank you Dad. *(Pause)* Ummm. Daddy? Haven't you forgotten something?

DAD For goodness sake. *(Finding a sixpenny piece from his trousers and giving it to* NIGEL*)* Here you go.

NIGEL Thanks Dad.

WARREL Bye Mr Slater.

DAD Five o'clock Nigel. We need to get the apples and carrots up to church for Sunday.

NIGEL Bye Dad. Come on then, where are we going?

WARREL Mr Dixon, then mine?

NIGEL This is Warrel. Warrel, meet everyone. Everyone meet Warrel.

WARREL Errr...hi.

NIGEL Warrel Blubb. That's his actual name. Warrel's my best friend. We walk to school together, we sit together, we walk back home afterwards, do our homework together, and every day after school we end up at his. On the way, though, we head to Mr Dixon's. *(Taking out a Parma Violet)* Most of my pocket money goes on sweets—

DAD What the bloody hell's that?

NIGEL A Parma Violet?

DAD Where did you get that from?

NIGEL Why?

DAD Parma Violets? What are you – they're a girl's sweet Nigel. You can't go around eating girls' sweets, what will people think? What you eat is incredibly important Nigel. Sweets are like – imagine I read the Mirror? Instead of the Telegraph. What would people think? You see? *(Leaving)* Parma Violets for a boy.

NIGEL If you thought Dad's rules of restaurants were complicated, sweets and chocolates are a whole new level. Watch this. *(We are suddenly in an episode of Top of the Form – WARREL is the contestant and NIGEL the question master)* Welcome to Top of the Form. Names?

PEGGY Peggy Longcroft.

WARREL Warrel Blubb.

JANICE Janice Parker.

NIGEL Team Captain Warrel Blubb, you will be answering questions on sweets and chocolates. First round, 'Mr Slater Says'. Are you ready?

WARREL I'm ready.

NIGEL Love Hearts.

WARREL Girls.

NIGEL Gobstoppers.

WARREL Boys.

NIGEL Rolos.

WARREL Boys. No, girls.

NIGEL It's boys. Milky Bars.

WARREL Boys.

NIGEL Sherbert Fountains. *(pause)* Come on, I need an answer..

WARREL Girls.

NIGEL Black Jacks.

WARREL Boys.

NIGEL Pear drops.

WARREL Girls.

NIGEL Apple bon bons. I'm going to have to press you.

WARREL Boys.

NIGEL Girls. Quality Street.

WARREL Everyone?

NIGEL Correct. Acid drops.

WARREL Boys.

NIGEL After Eights.

WARREL Parents.

NIGEL Quite right. *(smiling)* Parma Violets.

WARREL Girls.

NIGEL It's actually aunts. Flying Saucers.

WARREL Girls?

NIGEL Trick question – no one! Matchmakers.

WARREL Aunts again?

NIGEL It's parents. Traffic Lights.

WARREL Boys? No girls.

NIGEL It's boys! You see what I mean. Impossible! And then there are the Milky Bars and Club bars which you're not allowed to buy—

WARREL – but you can have if your parents have got them and you're at home—

NIGEL – True. And then barley sugars which your parents buy you for the car and which you can eat—

WARREL – but have to pretend not to like.

NIGEL And then, even if you know the rules, it doesn't mean you stick to them. I like acid drops – which are fine, chocolate limes – only just OK, and sherbet fountains –

WARREL – *Not* OK.

NIGEL *(taking a sweet from* **WARREL***'s bag)* Not OK but try sharing a sherbet fountain. Impossible—

WARREL – Oi! –

NIGEL – These, on the other hand? Impossible *not* to. Passes the boy test but fails the share test. Top tip. Don't buy bags of sweets. Sherbet fountains, or mars bars, or milky ways all the way. No one's ever going to ask to suck your liquorice stick are they?

WARREL Slater!

NIGEL Oh shut up!

We have arrived at the Blubb household.

MINNIE Language, Nigel.

WARREL Yeah, language *Nigel*.

NIGEL This is Warrel's Mum.

MINNIE Minnie. Minnie Blubb. How do you do? Right then bab, slippers on, and pass me your school blazer to brush. Oh, look at your hair *(licking her hand and smoothing* **WARREL**'s *hair)* – there we go.

NIGEL Warrel's teas are any schoolboy's dream – fish fingers with chips. Sausages and chips. Cadbury's Fingers, Jammie Dodgers, and Jaffa Cakes. He doesn't even offer me so much as a Bourbon. Bastard.

MINNIE Nigel Slater!

NIGEL Sorry Mrs Blubb.

MINNIE Right, off with you, bab you need to do your homework, and Nigel I'm sure your parents will be waiting for you for tea.

NIGEL I say goodbye, and head home to see what awaits, but as soon as I'm through the door I can hear my parents talking.

> **MUM** *and* **DAD** *are unaware that* **NIGEL** *has come in. He stops dead, to hear what is being said.*

MUM I can't Tony. Please.

DAD If that's what they say though, we'll have to think about it.

MUM I need to stay here. I need to be at home for Nigel.

DAD What about me?

MUM And you, obviously. I'll be able to cope, I promise.

DAD It's not the sort of thing you *can* promise.

MUM *(breaking)* Please don't make me.

DAD Let's see that the doctors say next time you go, OK? OK?

MUM OK.

DAD And if the worst comes to the worst –

MUM – It won't.

DAD But if it does. There's always care.

MUM Tony.

DAD It's not like it used to be. A lad at the factory and his wife put their baby in to care not long ago – they said it wasn't that bad at all.

NIGEL *(still outside of the action)* I guess that my mum's... pregnant and she doesn't want to have the baby in hospital. I like the idea of a little brother, or perhaps a sister. *(Beat, and then entering, brightly)* Hello.

MUM Nigel!

DAD How long have you been there?

NIGEL Not long, I just—

DAD You shouldn't listen in on other people's conversations Nigel.

NIGEL I—

MUM Tony. How are the Blubb's darling?

NIGEL Fine thank you.

DAD Help your mother bringing the things over.

NIGEL Lettuce, beetroot, cucumber, salad cream. We must be the only family in the country to put salad cream in a sauce boat. And ham. Ham's fine. But this is *not* ham. This is the sort of thing that you have to prise out of a green metal coffin, surrounded by brown jelly, the sort that ends up in evil, pink slices. *This* ham I *hate*. Why do they do this to me?

MUM You don't have to have salad cream if you don't want to.

DAD Ham?

NIGEL I think I'm OK actually Dad.

Pause. **DAD** *stabs his fork in to a slice of ham and slaps it on to* **NIGEL**'s *plate.*

DAD Eat that, it'll make you strong.

MUM I think he's OK Tony—

DAD Eat it!

(*Beat*).

– Don't *examine* it. *Eat* it.

(*Beat*).

MUM Tony, I think –

DAD Please.

Suddenly **DAD** *reaches over, grabs* **NIGEL**'s *plate, and throws it, ham salad going everywhere and the plate smashing.* **MUM** *is silent, shocked.* **DAD** *gets up and leaves, furious.* **NIGEL** *and* **MUM** *sit in silence.*

MUM Shall we have the gram on?

NIGEL What would you like?

MUM You choose.

NIGEL *has a look through the few records next to the gramophone. He finds one.*

NIGEL (*showing her*) This?

MUM Excellent choice.

NIGEL *puts it on – Charles Trenet's **"LA MER"** – and listens.*

Help me up.

NIGEL *goes over to* **MUM** *and helps her up. She holds out her hand.* **NIGEL** *looks at her, unsure of what to do.*

What, are you too old to dance with your mummy?

NIGEL *takes her hand, she brings him in to her and holds him. He hugs her tight.*

Now, put your left foot on my right foot. And then the other one. See? And then put this hand around me, and the other one you give me. Like that. See?

They dance, slowly, around the sitting room, MUM *leading the way. She's upset but trying to hide it from* NIGEL.

It's not long before you're going to be doing this with a girl of your own.

NIGEL *(embarassed)* Mum!

MUM What?

They continue to dance.

There's something I need to talk to you about, lamb chop. The thing is, you may need to start having your dinners at school. Just for while. Is that OK?

NIGEL Why's that?

MUM I just can't...it's a bit too much for me at the moment.

NIGEL Because of the...

MUM Yes. But it won't be for ever –

NIGEL It's OK Mum.

MUM Are you sure?

NIGEL Yes.

The continue to dance slowly, MUM *holding* NIGEL *tightly and trying to keep herself together.*

What's it called?

MUM What's that?

NIGEL What's this song called?

MUM 'La Mer'. It's French. Better not tell Auntie Fanny.

NIGEL What does it mean?

MUM The sea.

NIGEL It's nice.

MUM It's a great favourite. You can almost hear the light glittering and bouncing off the water. Listen.

They listen. At some point as NIGEL *talks the song ends.*

How about we have some Angel Delight for pudding?

NIGEL *beams.* MUM *goes to get the ingredients together.*

NIGEL Yes please. *(Picking up a packet to read, struggling over some of the words)* Modified starch, hydrogenated vegetable oil, emulsifiers, gelling agents, lactose, salt – and *magic*. One sachet emptied in to a half pint of milk and whisked for a minute and a half, left to set for five more. It might not be the most difficult thing in the world to make, but that doesn't matter. Butterscotch Angel Delight made by my mum – pure magic. I wish this would go on forever. I wish that Mum would always be mine and that I wouldn't have to share her.

The next morning I come downstairs and it's only Dad in the kitchen. Where's Mum?

DAD She's upstairs. She's getting up late today. I'm doing your breakfast. Sit down and I'll bring it over.

NIGEL Mum never gets up late. And Dad never makes my breakfast. If Mum was up she'd know to tell him that there are only two things I'll eat for breakfast. Sugar Puffs and Cap'n Crunch.

DAD *(putting down a bowl of porridge and a glass of hot Ribena in front of* NIGEL*)* Here you go.

NIGEL Ribena?! Everyone knows that I have orange squash for breakfast. And I don't like porridge. *(When he picks up his spoon, he starts pushing it around the bowl –* DAD *sits still and silently)* You can't eat it because it's too hot. And then you can't eat it because it's too cold. The only time you can eat it is the three minutes or so when it's perfect temperature. And then it just makes me want to be sick. I really don't want it, so I — (**DAD** *bites his bottom lip and then gets up and leaves)* He doesn't say anything, but somehow this is worse than last night.

The world changes and couple of months have passed. It is winter – an air of festivity, optimism floods the stage.

Welcome to my favourite time of year. Everywhere is white. It has snowed all night and the sky is a sort of grey-pink, the clouds look heavy, like they can't wait to snow some more. Cardboard boxes full of baubles and tinsel and tangled lights are brought down from the attic, and it's time for a trip to Percy Salt's. We go there throughout the year for everything from butter and kippers to sardines and eggs. But Christmas is a special trip, and –

MUM – and are you coming or not?

NIGEL I was just explaining –

MUM – Well could I suggest that you get a move on? Otherwise by the time we get there he'll be closed and there'll be nothing *to* explain.

NIGEL We leave Dad on the sofa, sitting in silence apart from the clock. He is concentrating all his efforts on eating a pomegranate with a tiny pin. He hasn't lost his mind, don't worry – this is a Christmas tradition for my father. He cuts the fruit in half around its tummy, sits it on a plate to catch the drips of juice, then sits quietly picking at the little red jewels. If there are pomegranates in the fruit bowl, Christmas can't be far away. Mum is getting shorter. Her back is arched, like she's carrying something that's too heavy for her all the time –

MUM Coat, Nigel!

NIGEL Yes Mother. *(Finding his coat and putting it on as they head out)* Percy W Salt. High class butcher and grocer – two parts of the same shop with a little secret stairway in the middle. Windows full of jars and boxes of everything you could hope to find on the left – legs of lamb and entire halves of cow hanging up on the right. I love it. *We* love it.

MUM Now, what do we need then, let's think.

NIGEL She knows exactly what we need, but making the list together is part of the fun. Turkish delight?

MUM In those sweet little wooden boxes, yes. Three should be fine.

NIGEL – The Turkish delight from Salt's is one of my favourite things *ever*. And crystallised figs.

MUM Absolutely. And sugared plums. And don't forget a couple of jars of cherries – the ones –

NIGEL – soaked in brandy. Sometimes I'm allowed to try one on Christmas Day. And how about the brandy for the butter?

MUM Oh yes, and don't forget the currants for the cake – I don't think we've got any left. Maybe some more butter for the mince pies, and a couple of cartons of icing sugar.

NIGEL And then the chocolate decorations for the tree.

MUM And wine. Six bottles of Mateus Rosé should see us through. Right. There we go then.

NIGEL And of course when we get back we've always picked *something* up that wasn't on the list – it's that sort of shop.

DAD Success?

MUM Yes, although he's getting terribly dear –

NIGEL – Expensive in normal language.

DAD Good good.

MUM Right. I suppose I had better *do* the cake. Are you going to help me?

NIGEL She knows I will. There are two Christmas traditions that will go on an on forever. First she'll make the Christmas cake – with my help of course –

MUM – Of course –

NIGEL – And when that's done, we'll repeat the process with the mince pies.

MUM Right then. Do you want to put on some carols? I'll find the recipes.

NIGEL Mum gets out the recipes – they're on blue Basildon Bond paper written in green biro and they're kept in the otherwise untouched Aga cookbook. I don't know how long Mum's had the recipes – for ever. They're the only two recipes she agrees to follow.

MUM So. Eight ounces of brown sugar. Eight of butter. Ten of plain flour. A half level teaspoon of cinnamon – and mixed spice. That's it more or less. Now, in to the bowl with the almonds, cherries, peel, sultanas and currants and raisins, brandy – *vitally* important – and then we stir.

NIGEL And then in to the prepared cake tins –

MUM Oh heck –

NIGEL – The prepared cake tins that Mum has once again forgotten to prepare. Cue desperate scramble for the brown greaseproof paper, scissors and –

MUM – Where's the string?

NIGEL Here we go.

MUM – Right. And in to the prepared cake tins we go.

NIGEL Mum spoons it in to the tins –

MUM – Shhh, listen to the cake mixture.

Pause as they listen.

NIGEL And then in to the oven. Every home should smell of baking Christmas cake. *(Pause)* Flapjacks. Old books. Snow.

Roast chicken. Moss. Cress seeds sprouting on blotting paper. Jam tarts... Baking Christmas cake. Mum. When the cake is out of the oven and cooled, and as always sunk in the middle –

MUM – Nothing some extra marzipan won't cover up. Right, the icing.

NIGEL The Slater look is...interesting. Icing sugar on the table, floor, me – and a cake that ends up looking a bit like an unmade bed with folds and lumps and creases and tears, and extra odd patches stuck on with a apricot jam –

MUM Do you want to do it this year?

NIGEL Pardon?

MUM Oh I've had enough of the icing lark, dear. You're old enough now. Why don't you have a go?

NIGEL It's your thing though –

MUM Don't be daft. You have a go. Just remember, you're going for snowy peaks.

NIGEL Mum goes in to the other room to sit down. She's started sitting down a lot. I've seen pictures of Christmas cakes before – smooth and perfectly iced. I try.

He takes a knife and goes around the cake with it, covering the layer of marzipan with icing. When he's finished he steps back to look at it.

Perfect. Like...like it's snowed all night and you're the first person outside and it's just...perfect. And I know that I can't leave it like that. I can hear Mum coming back. I take the knife and start bringing bits up all around the cake just as –

MUM Not bad at all darling. Well done. Don't forget Father Christmas and the tree.

NIGEL *puts the decorations on top of the cake.*

There we go. Perfect.

NIGEL The cake will sit pride of place on the table throughout Christmas dinner. After the turkey's devoured, after the roast potatoes and parsnips are gone, the cake will still be there. On Boxing Day when Dad makes his turkey stew –

DAD – Fricassee if you don't mind.

NIGEL When Dad makes his turkey *fricassee*. After he's stripped the bones and cut them into small chunks, each small bit of meat rescued from the bird a personal triumph. And after he's cooked it and cooked it and cooked it some more with onions and red peppers, some red spice powder and a bay leaf –

DAD – Don't swallow the bay leaf! –

NIGEL – Dad will joke, *every* year. And after he's cooked it until it's turned in to a thick, brick-coloured stew, and no one's choked on a bay leaf, the cake will still be there. When was Christmas ever Christmas without having to wonder what to do with the leftover cake in mid-January? Mince pies, though, never last long. Alongside jam tarts, mince pies are my favourite thing to make. Mum?

MUM Get the rolling pin out then, let's get them done. Can you remember what we need?

NIGEL Ummm. Ten ounces of flour.

MUM Tick.

NIGEL Four ounces of butter.

MUM Tick.

NIGEL And the magic ingredient. One ounce of lard.

MUM Tick.

NIGEL Ummm... *(Struggling)*

MUM Sugar?

NIGEL Two! Two tablespoons of caster—

MUM – Teaspoons –

NIGEL Teaspoons. Two teaspoons of caster sugar.

MUM Tick.

NIGEL And... *(Struggling again)*

MUM Eggs?—

NIGEL – An egg yolk!

MUM Tick.

NIGEL And last but not least – a pound of mincemeat – more or less. I take out the old tins, and wipe them clean. I sift. I rub the tiny cubes of cold butter and lard into the flour. I knead and Mum starts to roll the pastry out. She concentrates so hard, like it's a maths problem at school. She really wants to get it done, I can tell, but after a while she – and so I take over and Mum goes to sit down on the kitchen stool with her inhaler. I carry on rolling the pastry, and then cut the little cases out with our red plastic crinkle-edged cutter. And –

During the following it becomes clear that things aren't going according to plan – NIGEL *isn't sticking to his lines, and* MUM *and potentially other members of the company have realised. They might come on to the stage to see what's happening – they may check a script to find out what's going on.*

MUM – Nigel –

NIGEL – And then I push them down into the little grooves in the tins. And—

MUM – Darling –

NIGEL – we fill them to the brim with mincemeat. Mince pies aren't like jam tarts – you have to pack them tight. And then their little pastry tops go on, and –

MUM – And that's not what happened is it?

Pause.

NIGEL What?

MUM That's not what happened, Nigel. That's not what's written in the script. *(Pause)* Shall we go back a little bit? *(Further pause – going back in the script a few lines)* Nigel? Can you remember what we need?

NIGEL Ummm. Ten ounces of flour.

MUM Tick.

NIGEL Four ounces of butter.

MUM Tick.

NIGEL And the magic ingredient. One ounce of lard.

MUM Tick.

NIGEL Ummm... *(Struggling)*

MUM Sugar?

NIGEL Two! Two tablespoons of caster—

MUM – Teaspoons –

NIGEL Teaspoons. Two teaspoons of caster sugar.

MUM Tick.

NIGEL And... *(Struggling again)*

MUM Eggs?—

NIGEL – An egg yolk!

MUM Tick.

NIGEL And last but not least – a pound of mincemeat.

MUM Ummmm... *(Searching for the mincemeat)* Oh, what a nuisance – I must have forgotten to put it on the shopping list for—

NIGEL Mum?

MUM It's OK, I'll get some from the shops tomorrow.

NIGEL But Mummy, you *promised* we could –

MUM – Darling I'm sorry. I must have assumed we had some in the larder and I forgot to check –

NIGEL – I knew you'd forget. I *knew* it! You're hopeless. You never do *anything* right! I hope you *die*! *(Pause)* And I run up stairs to my room, and I slam the door and throw myself onto the bed. And – and then it's the middle of the night. And I'm awake. I'm awake because – well, who can sleep so close to Christmas Eve? I'm snuggled down under the sheets, pulled up tight around my ears. Toasty. I can see little bits of ice around the edges of my window – it must be so frosty outside. Christmas morning means my stocking – which is actually a pillowcase, with a chocolate selection box in the shape of an actual stocking inside it. I'm sure Christmas is going to be amazing this year. With Mum so poorly, Father Christmas will make sure she has a good time. I go and see if he's been early by any chance. I push back my sheets, and get out of my warm cocoon, and I pad downstairs. *(Pause)* And there's no stocking. There are no presents and no ribbons. There are no clementines and there's no Cadbury's Selection Box. There's just Mum's Christmas cake on the table, and Dad. On the floor. And I know that Father Christmas isn't coming. And I know I'm not getting a brother or sister. And I know that everything in the world is about to change.

Lights down, leaving a spotlight on the Christmas cake.

ACT TWO

The spotlight on the Christmas cake remains. Lights up on NIGEL, *on his own, lonely, in a black suit, shirt untucked, without shoes perhaps, reading the same cookbook as he started the play with. We are still at home in Wolverhampton.*

NIGEL *(showing the audience and reading out as appropriate)* Marguerite Patten on vegetables. A for asparagus. Wash carefully, then cut off a little of the thick white base of stalks. Boil in salted water for twenty to twenty-five minutes. B for Brussel sprouts – disgusting. Mark a cross with a sharp knife at the base of each sprout. Boil rapidly like cabbage – C. D is for—

DAD *enters in a tuxedo and a rush.*

Dad.

DAD Have you seen my tie? And why aren't you ready?

NIGEL Sorry. E is for...Dad, do you like... endive?

DAD No one actually eats that, Nigel – that's just cookery book nonsense – have you seen my tie?

NIGEL No, sorry –

DAD – Bloody hell – look, Nigel, can you get ready please? *(Leaving)* We can't be late.

NIGEL *(going back to the book)* F is for... *(To the audience)* Auntie Fanny's been in a home for the last few months now. She had a fall, and with Mum not around Dad said he couldn't cope any more. She's alright, and we see her, but... *(DAD comes back in again, having found his tie)* Dad have you had fennel before? Apparently it's particularly good with fish and can be served with a white sauce –

DAD Not now, Nigel. Right, we're off.

NIGEL *(getting ready, then with a sense of realisation, to the audience)* Just to be clear, this isn't Mum's...funeral. This is Ladies' Night at the Masons. The Masons have always been a big thing with Dad, with their rolled up left trouser legs and their sticking their hands up like they know the answer to something no one asked. Since Mum though, he's been going all the time. And most weeks, I go too. *(Beat)* I didn't go to the funeral. I didn't even know it was happening –

Some time before.

DAD – Aunt Elvie and Uncle Len will be over in a bit. Remember to say –

NIGEL – Yes, please –

DAD – and –

NIGEL – Thank you? –

DAD – Just be polite. And I'll be back in time to tuck you in later. OK?

   AUNT ELVIE *and* **UNCLE LEN** *enter, joining* **NIGEL** *at the table.*

NIGEL Dinner that evening is...silent. Tomato soup and lamb chops and not a *word*. I eat as slowly as I can.

LEN Thank you dear, that was delicious, under the circumstances. Nigel?

NIGEL Thank you Aunt Elvie.

ELVIE Pudding? How about some Christmas cake?

NIGEL No!... Thank you.

ELVIE Len?

LEN Goodness, no, I couldn't.

ELVIE Nigel?

NIGEL No thank you.

ELVIE No. Come to think of it... *(She takes the Christmas cake and throws it away)* Probably for the best. Right. You go and do the dishes and Nigel you go and get ready for bed, your father will be back to say goodnight.

Beat. **NIGEL** *stares at the place where the cake used to be. He leaves the table, taking out a folded sheet of paper from his jacket.*

NIGEL *(reading)* "Food". A poem, by Nigel Slater.

A slice of pie in July is nice.

Like bread and butter pudding in winter, and cuddling.

Like goodnights from my mummy.

My head on my pillow,

her kiss soft like a marshmallow.

More than her hugs, her cuddles, her good night and sleep tight, more than all of that put together, I miss my goodnight kiss from Mum.

NIGEL *goes to get in to bed. He sees two pink marshmallows on the bedside table.* **DAD** *enters.*

For me?

DAD Of course. I know they're your favourites. Good night Nigel.

NIGEL And as I go to bed tonight and every night for the next two years, there are two soft, pink marshmallows on the bedside table. *(Beat)* Of course they're not my favourite, and of course they're nothing like the real thing, but it's all Dad can do. Since Mum it's like he's wearing a coat that's too big for him. He's stopped having all of his favourite things – tripe and onions, even his — *(Coming in to* **DAD** *with some mushrooms)* Dad, look what I got.

DAD Not now Nigel.

NIGEL I thought I could do your fried mushrooms for you.

DAD You'll mess up the Aga.

NIGEL I'll be careful, I promise.

DAD Just leave it, Nigel, please.

NIGEL So now it's cheese on toast, spaghetti hoops, baked potatoes and more spaghetti hoops. We only use two pans in the kitchen now – if you move any of the others tiny little silver things shoot out from underneath. Cadbury Mini Rolls have replaced Mum's pancakes and apple crumbles. I never thought it would be possible to get bored of Mini Rolls.

DAD Mini Rolls?

NIGEL is confused, struggling, in a daze, and we are back at Lady's Night at the Masons. DAD is trying to get his attention as the world of the past few weeks transforms in to a Masonic lodge, with flower displays and women in ballgowns entering.

Nigel. Nigel! What's got in to you? Come on.

NIGEL *(still dazed)* Sorry. I...

DAD There we are then. *(Seeing two women – MRS E. and JOAN)* Mrs Everard. Mrs Potter.

MRS E. Tony. How are you? I'm so sorry –

JOAN – And this must be Nigel?

DAD It is indeed. Nigel. Say hello to Mrs Potter and Mrs Everard –

NIGEL It turns out adults talk to you differently when your mum has died. Like you're made of glass – or you're just stupid.

MRS E. – Oh no, call me Eunice. Oh darling, how are you bearing up you poor little poppet?

JOAN How do.

NIGEL At least *most* adults do. How do you do?

MRS E. Shall we? Tony? Joan?

DAD Go and wash your hands, Nigel.

They move towards their table, sitting down.

NIGEL Roast chicken is followed by strawberries and cream, which come in a massive sundae dish, sprinkled with sugar and with the cream piled up on top of strawberries that seem, well—

JOAN – Green!

MRS E. I knew they wouldn't be ripe. *(Eating one)* Oh goodness they're sour.

NIGEL Sour or not, I dig in. And soon more and more dishes are making their way my way.

MRS E. *(conspiratorially, laughing)* I bet you can't eat them *all*!

NIGEL *(to the audience)* I bet I *can*. Coffee is served, and I'm still going. And then everyone is leaving, and I'm still going. And the waiters are taking off the tablecloths and the room is being swept, and I'm still there, stuffing green strawberries. *(Beat)* It turns out a wash hand basin can take a *lot* of sick. But not *enough*.

JOAN You might have at least pulled the sink plug out first.

NIGEL I'm sorry, I—

JOAN Revolting.

NIGEL I'm half asleep in the back of Dad's car on the way home, the car stinking of sick and strawberries and anger. I don't go to Ladies' Night again. And it turns out my luck with strawberries is *nothing* compared to my success with raspberries.

We are back at home.

Dad?

DAD Nigel.

NIGEL You know what it is in three days' time?

DAD Friday.

NIGEL *Dad!*

DAD What? It's Friday. *(Handing* **NIGEL** *a bowl of raspberries)* Here you go.

NIGEL You're hopeless Father. Can I take mine in the other room?

DAD If you're very careful – there's a lot of juice in there.

NIGEL *(taking the bowl in to the living room)* Raspberries are probably the best fruit there is. Better than peaches, better than apricots, and since Ladies' Night, even strawberries.

He puts the bowl on the footstool and drags it across the room. It hits something and the bowl bounces off the footstool. Time slows down as **NIGEL** *realises what has happened.*

No, no, no.

The bowl is upside down and the juice is spreading out everywhere, the stain getting bigger by the second.

I walk in to the kitchen as calmly as I can. Dad where's the dishcloth please?

DAD Nigel? You haven't?

NIGEL Dad—

DAD – You *haven't?*

DAD walks in to the sitting room and sees the mess.

(grabbing the dishcloth) Give it here!

NIGEL *(swallowing his apology)* Sorry Daddy.

DAD gets down and starts to try to clean the mess, but it's hopeless. He puts the dish and dishcloth on the floor and comes back up. He grabs NIGEL *by the back of his collar and slaps him across the face.*

DAD I *told* you to be careful! I *told* you.

He can't stop slapping NIGEL *across the face,* NIGEL *falls,* DAD *grabs him back up and hits him again, harder and harder. He can't stop –* NIGEL *pleading, apologising,* DAD *shouting, until they both collapse on the floor together.* DAD *gathers himself and leaves, leaving* NIGEL *alone.*

(calling) Joan. Could you?

JOAN *enters – she gets down on to the floor and starts to clean up the mess.*

JOAN Bleedin' hell.

NIGEL I'm not sure quite when Mrs Potter started as our cleaner. I only know that she did. Apparently Dad met her at a disabled charity where she volunteers. Four raffles, three whist drives and one sink-related strawberry incident later, here she is. In three days' time it *is* Friday. But the good news is that it's also my thirteenth birthday.

DAD *(calling)* Nigel?

NIGEL Dad? What are you doing back?

DAD I cancelled a potentially very boring meeting – I heard it was a certain someone's birthday. I thought we could go you know where.

NIGEL *(beaming)* I *do* know where. Where is shelves stacked to the roof with jars, so big that the shopkeeper can hardly get her hand round to unscrew them. Where is the sweet shop. Sweets for everyone. Barley sugars, éclairs, mint humbugs, pear drops, buttered Brazils for Dad, jelly babies, liquorice torpedos—

DAD – What would you like then?

NIGEL Easy! Refreshers.

DAD Excellent. Anything else?

NIGEL Love Hearts please.

DAD Some Love Hearts please. And one more, Nigel?

NIGEL Ummmm. Fairy drops please.

DAD You can choose whatever you want.

NIGEL I know, you just said. I just chose! Fairy drops please.

DAD *Anything* at all. Peanut brittle? Rolos?

NIGEL Ummm, no I'm fine with fairy drops please—

DAD Don't keep *on* saying it, Nigel.

NIGEL What's wrong with saying fairy—

DAD Enough Nigel. We'll have some of...them please. And that'll be everything. Right, come on you nancy boy. *(Leaving* NIGEL *eating sweets)*

NIGEL Dad is starting to make me nervous. First Mrs Potter. Then not being allowed 'fairy drops'. Now eggs. He might not read *books*, but he reads the Telegraph, and he's been making a point of showing me the Egg Marketing Board adverts recently. More specifically, it's Sam, a freckly boy sitting at the kitchen table grinning as he attacks a boiled egg with a spoon. It's like they're jumping out of the paper and in to our sitting room just to spite me.

The ADVERTS *come to life.*

AD 1 Go to work on an egg—

AD 2 Go to work on an egg and be your best all day!

AD 1 Sam says –

SAM I like boiled eggs not too runny and not too hard.

AD 2 Sam says

SAM Guess what day we have fried eggs for breakfast. Give up? Fri-day! Get it?

NIGEL I think we all got it. Would you mind if we –

AD 1 Four minutes to boil—

AD 2 Two minutes to fry—

ADS AND SAM – Three minutes to eat.

AD 1 Protein, iron *and* vitamins. Those few minutes are vitally important to your whole day's health and happiness.

AD 2 Your delicious fried egg has the precise iron and vitamins to last you all morning, and to make your whole day better and happier.

SAM You feel nourished, and your very best.

AD 2 It's so little time and trouble to have an egg – or two – for breakfast, with so much reward!

NIGEL OK that's –

AD 1 – Go to work on an egg –

SAM – Be your best all day –

NIGEL – That's enough, thank you!

ADS AND SAM *(leaving)* – Eggs!

NIGEL If you can see a healthy, sporty boy who can't eat enough eggs and a spotty nancy boy who won't eat *any*, it doesn't take a genius to work out that eggs are the answer. And so Dad *has* worked it out. But here's the thing. I *hate* eggs. Whatever they look like. Poached, boiled, fried, scrambled, omeletted, salad sandwiched, hidden under baked beans – *all* of which Dad has tried. I mean I really, truly, *hate* them. This isn't a new thing – the problem is, Mum has always covered for me. Whenever an egg –

DAD *(entering, placing a plate in front of* **NIGEL***)* – Here we go then. A breakfast for champions –

NIGEL – Thank you. Whenever an egg came anywhere near me, she was there, making something up to get me out of it. And now she's not here, but *this* is. Dad I think I'm feeling ill –

DAD Come on –

NIGEL – Queasy?

DAD Nigel –

NIGEL – Sick, Dad, I feel very sick –

DAD Just *try* it, Nigel, please. You have to eat *something* for breakfast – you'll faint otherwise.

NIGEL I eat the bacon and sausage as slowly as possible, giving enough time for, I don't know...the end of the world? A dog to find its way in to the kitchen, jump up on to my lap and save me? For Dad to...drop dead? It's looking at me. The disgusting white around some sort of yellow fudge, covered in a skin that's shrinking by the minute. And I just can't—

DAD – *Eat* it.

   (Beat).

   – Open your mouth –

NIGEL – Please Dad—

DAD – Open now or I promise I'll hit you.

   NIGEL *opens his mouth and* DAD *puts the fork in – he tries to chew and swallow but he can't. Shaking his head, eyes screwed tight,* DAD *holding his neck he starts to squeal,* DAD *keeping him sat down. Finally he gets out, running away to be sick.*

NIGEL *(recovering)* Dad doesn't try to make me eggs again. And I'm left – the front door closing just a little bit too loudly, the car starting – Dad gone. And I'm on my own, in a big creaky, wooden-panelled house. (Beat) I go across the landing to Dad's bedroom. The last time I tried to open the door – the day Mum died – it banged against her oxygen tank. It smells of Mum. Not her perfume, or her lipstick, or her clothes or her inhaler – just her. There's a small plate with a part-nibbled digestive next to Dad's side of the bed. Mum's favourites. She didn't nibble though. She dunked. She said the perfect dunking biscuit –

MUM – will always stay intact. No matter how long you dip it. It won't collapse –

NIGEL – like a rich tea or a digestive.

MUM – Even if you pause, mid-dunk, for a particularly eyebrow-raising story at a coffee morning, it holds its shape.

JOAN *(calling)* Nigel. Where are –

NIGEL *isn't ready.*

Say the other thing about digestives?

MUM Digestives might not be suited to dunking, they do always manage to taste of home. They have a unique ability to take you to a safe place, to somewhere you think you remember fondly, even though you may never have been there. They're wheaty, sweet, with a—

NIGEL – with a hint of the hamster's cage about them.

MUM Exactly. Now go on, you'd better go downstairs.

NIGEL I—

MUM Go on.

JOAN *(calling)* Nigel?

NIGEL I can't understand how we got here, how things can have changed *this* much, in no time at all. Little do I know that things are going to get a whole lot worse in even less time at all.

JOAN *(calling)* Where are you?

NIGEL I'm just – I'm –

JOAN Well *just* get down here and help me will you? Make yourself useful.

NIGEL Mrs Potter *lives* to clean.

JOAN Dirt gets on my nerves –

NIGEL – must come out of her mouth at least seventy-five times a day. She cleans in places that I didn't even know a brush or a cloth could get to.

JOAN You can tell a lot about a person Nigel. You can be as polite as you please, as lah-de-dah as can be, it doesn't matter one bit if you've not polished your brass. A spotless lav goes a long way in this world. You see here? Most people wouldn't even *think* to clean in there.

NIGEL She enjoys cleaning – *enjoys* cleaning – the same way Dad enjoys gardening. It's nearly six o'clock and she's attacking an old wooden mirror.

JOAN, hair in rollers, alternating hands between cigarette and mug of coffee, is scouring an old wooden mirror frame.

It's been in the house for ever, and Mum used to love it.

JOAN And I'm going to do take a brillo to the pans tomorrow.

DAD enters, holding a small package, seeing JOAN at the frame.

DAD Oh, Joan, actually that was supposed to look like that.

JOAN Oh well. It looked absolutely –

NIGEL – filthy –

JOAN – Exactly. It looked filthy to me, so –

NIGEL *(sensing that something's wrong)* Dad?

DAD Nigel. Auntie Fanny – she died today I'm afraid. *(Giving him the package)* This was left for you under her bed.

JOAN What is it?

DAD I haven't opened it.

Beat. NIGEL starts to walk away from JOAN and DAD, to open the package on his own. As he leaves –.

JOAN I don't see what the fuss is about. You said she was a revolting woman.

NIGEL *is on his own. He opens that package and pours out the contents in to his hand – packets and packets of Parma Violets.*

Some time later.

NIGEL One day I come home and find her sat in Auntie Fanny's old chair. Even thought it's been re-done in a different colour, it still smells of – well, Auntie Fanny. But she's sitting there just the same, darning Dad's socks. Wouldn't it just be cheaper for Dad to buy some more?

JOAN It may well be cheaper young man. But not everything's about money. It just happens that I'm doing this because I want to. I don't like the idea of him walking around with holes in his socks. Now hadn't you better go and clean your room?

NIGEL I go up to my room, furious. What has it got to do with her if *my* Dad walks around with holes in his –

DAD *(calling)* Nigel.

NIGEL What?

DAD Get ready, we're going for a ride in the car.

NIGEL Pardon?

DAD You heard me, get ready. We're going for a drive.

NIGEL An hour later we're following signs for Worcester, and suddenly I realise. Dad, are we visiting Auntie Betty? She says 'bugger' and 'shit' and I love it because Dad gets so embarrassed he has to look at his shoes.

DAD Well yes and no.

NIGEL I've found that whenever parents or teachers or any adults say 'Well yes and no' it means mostly 'no' with a tiny bit of 'yes' that doesn't change it being 'no'.

DAD Do you remember saying how much you like it at Auntie Betty's?

NIGEL *(to the audience)* I remember saying I like Auntie Betty – and her house because she's there.

DAD Well she decided that it was a bit big for her and so she's moved to Hereford. And so we've bought the house. I wanted it to be a surprise.

NIGEL The house is Clayford. At the top of a Ankerdine Hill, which basically should be called Ankerdine Mountain, it's that steep. At the bottom of the hill is Knightwick, a tiny little village with fields full of sheep and horses and cows, and a river where you can swim. It's not a bad place to spend your holidays.

DAD We've already managed to get you in to the local school –

NIGEL What?

DAD The school in Martley, it's the next village across – they've already said you can go there.

Pause.

NIGEL I –

DAD What is it?

NIGEL I thought you mean't –

DAD *(handing* **NIGEL** *a bag of sweets)* Here, have one of these. They're your favourites.

NIGEL Chocolate eclairs *aren't* my favourites. Chocolate *toffees* are my favourite. It couldn't be any more different from Wolverhampton. We turn on to the gravel road that leads to the house.

DAD You like Mrs Potter, don't you?

NIGEL I – *(To the audience)* I don't know what to say. I –

DAD – Doesn't she remind you of Mummy?

Pause.

NIGEL There's nothing I *can* say. I could say that when I came home the other day and she was wearing Mum's apron, *all* I could think of was that she wasn't anything like Mum. But I can't say that. So I say nothing. And the car crunches to a stop and –

DAD You know, you could call her Auntie Joan — if you wanted?

JOAN You've arrived! Come in – I've made a cake. I'll put the kettle on. *(To* **DAD***)* Did you –

DAD Yes. Nigel?

JOAN Did your dad say? You can call me Auntie Joanie if you want?

> **NIGEL** *looks at her, walks straight past her, into the kitchen where in front of him is a perfect looking homemade apple pie.*

NIGEL Does she remind me of Mum? Not one bit.

JOAN *(to* **DAD***)* I told you –

DAD – Give him time. He'll be fine.

NIGEL One thing he will *not* be is fine. *(Beat)* There's nothing good about Clayford as a house. For a start, it's on top of a massive hill – did I mention that? Which means we're miles from anywhere. The layout doesn't work either. I have to walk through Dad's bedroom to get to mine. You can hear everything going on in both rooms. *Everything.* And with the move Mrs Potter — Auntie... *Joan's* cleaning has got worse. At home she at least used to clean things that mattered like floors and tables and things. Now she's just obsessed with polishing.

JOAN *(manically finding items, inspecting them, polishing them. Firstly a large copper pan)* Oh, what's this? Lovely. Horseshoes! Tony there are horseshoes! Now these are filthy *(picking up some coal tongs)* – you are in need of some serious attention tomorrow aren't you.

NIGEL The woman has lost it. The only thing worse than Clayford and her horseshoes is Chantry – my new school. Probably the scariest two words in the world. Even scarier than "Auntie Joanie". And all the worse when it coincides with just having moved halfway across the country and knowing a grand total of zero people.

We are transported to Chantry. Enter MICHAEL *and* TRACEY.

MICHAEL I'm Michael. And this is Tracey.

TRACEY And I'm Tracey.

NIGEL Hello. I'm Nigel.

TRACEY And I'm Tracey.

NIGEL Hi Tracey, I'm Nigel.

MICHAEL I live at Spetchley Farm and my brother works at Longlands. Tracey's dad owns Longlands.

TRACEY That's my dad. He owns it.

MICHAEL That's what I just said.

TRACEY Well then.

MICHAEL Tracey's not so clever.

TRACEY Where do you live Ronald?

MICHAEL *Ronald?*

NIGEL It's Nigel.

TRACEY Where do you live then Niall?

MICHAEL *Nigel!* Like I said about Tracey.

NIGEL Ankerdine Hill?

   Pause.

MICHAEL I didn't know there were any farms up that way?

NIGEL There aren't.

MICHAEL So – your parents...work on a farm somewhere else?

NIGEL No. My mum's – she died. And my dad has a factory that does parts for cars?

MICHAEL Oh.

TRACEY My rabbit got run over last May.

NIGEL These are my school friends – which turn out to be exactly that. When I go home each day I don't see anyone until the next morning. In the summer holidays I see no one but Dad and Joan for six weeks.

A bell rings for lunchtime.

MICHAEL Lunch roulette! What do you think today? Shepherd's pie, fish pie, cheese pie or cottage pie?

TRACEY I like pie.

NIGEL It turns out today we're not so lucky. The number one rule of pudding is that whatever it is has to be sweet – a treat. Anything that is sloppy, or slimy, or gummy, or lumpy, makes you gag or retch or heave can't be a pudding. So what I'd like to know is how come anyone ever thought it was OK to have tapioca as a pudding?

MICHAEL What do we think for afters?

TRACEY It's always sponge after stew. Or tart. Jam tart. Or treacle tart. I like tart.

MICHAEL Ohhh, treacle. Please let it be treacle. *(To* NIGEL*)* It's really good. They do it with a layer of breadcrumbs on top and a golden syrup criss-cross thing with the pastry.

NIGEL It turns out today we're not so lucky. The number one rule of pudding is that whatever it is has to be a sweet, a treat, something nice that you want and most importantly something you'll agree to be good for. Anything that is sloppy, or slimy, or gummy, or lumpy, makes you gag or retch or heave *can't* be a pudding. So what I'd like to know is how come anyone *ever* thought it was OK to have tapioca as a pudding?

Tapioca is being ladled out in to bowls and passed down the table.

Not for me thank you. I'm full.

TRACEY You have to eat it – it's the rules.

NIGEL Michael is wolfing his down like he thinks its treacle or chocolate sponge, like he's forgotten it's basically porridge with old man bogeys in it.

TRACEY They'll just check your bowl and they won't let you leave the table.

MICHAEL Just eat it.

NIGEL I can't. *(Whispering)* Michael?

MICHAEL Yes?

NIGEL Would you like mine?

MICHAEL Go on then.

NIGEL Luckily the food at Clayford is far better. In summer tinned salmon and cucumber salad with new potatoes. In winter, boiled gammon with a thick parsley sauce, spinach and mashed –

JOAN –Creamed if you don't mind –

NIGEL – *(mouthing)* mashed potato. Every house smells of something. Ours smells of boiled ham and parsley sauce. The parsley used to come out of a jar, but now it comes from Dad, who's started growing rows of it in the garden. As the ham slowly boils in the pan of water –

JOAN – Get the butter Nigel.

NIGEL – *(going to get the butter)* As the ham's nearly ready Joan prepares the mash –

JOAN – creamed! –

NIGEL – creamed potatoes. Mushing the sauce in to the creamy clouds of potato is good enough but nothing comes close to the first forkful of ham with thick green sauce. Other times she does a stew, and then every now and again we have a mixed grill, with a small piece of steak, an opened up kidney, a bit of lamb's liver, tomatoes, black pudding and a sausage on an oval plate –

DAD *suddenly clutches his chest, in pain.*

NIGEL Dad –

DAD It's, I'm fine. Just wait a second.

JOAN He's fine – he just needs some exercise.

DAD I'm in the garden all the time.

JOAN That's not the same thing and you know it. *(To* **NIGEL***)* Your Father's going to be taking up tennis though. Aren't you Tony.

DAD Apparently.

JOAN Right then. Now, deep breathes. I'll get the afters.

She leaves and returns moments later with an apple pie and custard.

NIGEL Tennis?

DAD Two sessions a week.

JOAN Right, here we go.

DAD Are you trying to get rid of me? I can't eat all of this –

JOAN – Don't be silly Tony, of course you can. *(Serving it up)* Whoever said they couldn't manage a home-made apple pie?

NIGEL You'll have to start having brown bread toast too.

DAD That's enough from you.

JOAN Custard?

A bells goes – we are back at school. Enter **MISS A.** *She will address the audience as the class.*

MISS A Curdle. Separate. Split. Collapse. Four words that should from this day forth forever strike the fear of God in to you. Can anyone tell me what we would associate with these words? Halward?

No answer.

Portman?

Still no answer.

Is anyone awake today? Slater?

NIGEL Sorry miss.

MISS A Useless. Curdle, separate, split and collapse – four words we would associate with custard.

NIGEL Welcome to Wednesday afternoon cookery lessons with Miss Adams.

MISS A We live in a world of tins. Tinned meat. Tinned fruit. Tinned custard. Resist it. We shall start with something nice and simple – a Victoria Sandwich.

NIGEL And so we start. Raspberry jam, made from scratch –

MISS A – Always makes sure it sets. It needs to be stiff. So stiff that you could turn the jar upside down and contents stay put. As stiff as – what else? *(Pause)* As stiff as – *(beat)*– filthy minds.

NIGEL After the jam the sponge. Mine rises like a dream, and –

MISS A – Good crumb, Slater, good crumb.

NIGEL I'm not quite sure what that means but I'm assuming it's good because she's let me take mine home and not thrown it in the bin like Tracey and Michael's. I put it in a biscuit tin, in to my bag, and start back home. I can't wait to show Dad. *(Reaching home)* Dad. Auntie Joan. Drumroll please. *(He takes the lid off the tin to show the cake off)*

DAD *(proudly)* Well would you look at that. Isn't a beauty Joan?

JOAN Hmm.

NIGEL The next Wednesday when I get back home from cookery class with red, bloody-looking fingers after a lesson in chutneyed beetroot, there it is, on the kitchen table. The *perfect* Victoria sandwich. Three inches high, a thin line of apricot jam in the middle—

JOAN Your father seems to prefer it when I use apricot jam instead of raspberry – it's just a little less tart I find.

NIGEL The top is dusted with caster sugar, and even the criss-cross of the cooling rack is etched on the soft, golden top.

JOAN Just something I rustled up earlier today – would you like a slice young man?

Beat. A moment of realisation.

NIGEL Every Wednesday from then on without fail, sponges and fruitcakes, cream éclairs, Battenberg cakes – which she calls church window cake for no reason apart from to be difficult – jams and preserves, pies, tarts, even soups, make their way on to the kitchen table, our own Ankerdine Hill demilitarised zone, with just one purpose. To impress Dad. This week, a decisive, devious damson jam move from Slater –

DAD Damsons? My absolutely favourite, how lovely –

NIGEL Pure coincidence of course. *(To* **DAD***)* As soon as I get back though, I can tell something's up. Lawn perfectly clear of leaves. Bright yellow, maroon and white dahlias in a jar on the table. And the smell of baking – like a blanket you just want to wrap yourself in, hanging in the air.

NIGEL *comes rushing in with his jar of jam.*

JOAN Oh. What's this then?

NIGEL Damson jam. From the garden.

JOAN That's nice. I've never really got on with damsons. Are you hungry? I've just been rustling up a few bits and bobs while you've been at school. I've just made some jam tarts, lemon curd tarts, butterfly cakes, mince pies, an apple sponge, a mandarin orange and cherry pavlova, and, oh yes, I nearly forgot – these.

One large lemon meringue pie appears alongside the other 'bits and bobs' JOAN *has prepared, as well as a perfect, individual mini lemon meringue pie for everyone in the audience.*

NIGEL Welcome to a new, deadly phase in the Cold War. Welcome to the Battle of Clayford. On the one side, Nigel Slater, a teenager with a strong crumb. On the other, Joan Potter, a chain-smoking bitch with a Pledge problem. Joan's lemon meringue pie is a brutal, blatant, act of war, and one of the most amazing things I've ever put in my mouth. Five lemons' worth of sharpness, served warm, probably the lightest pastry I have ever tasted, all topped with a thick, sweet hat of meringue. It's not even her recipe, she got it from her daughter, but I'm still desperate to find out how to make it. Whenever I ask though –

JOAN – Shouldn't be doing your homework? –

NIGEL – Or, more annoyingly—

JOAN – A magician never reveals how his trick works does he? –

NIGEL – or finally, most recently, Joan just plain lying to my face—

JOAN – I can't remember to be honest. It just comes in to my head once I get started.

NIGEL Whatever the recipe is, it's a decisive victory.

JOAN Look forward to seeing what you've got up your sleeve next Wednesday, Little Miss Cookery Class. What sort of a boy even makes damson jam? *(Leaving)* If you were any sort of a lad at all you'd be out there helping your father chop logs rather than flouncing around with fruit pies and the like.

NIGEL *gathers himself, stunned at* JOAN*'s attack.*

NIGEL I think Dad honestly believes he has created some sort of storybook happy family. *(Taking out his notebook and starts to make a list)* A list of things I'd like to tell Dad, by Nigel Slater.

As NIGEL *starts to rant, he'll circle, making advances on the lemon meringue pie, which seems to be taunting him. A few times he'll go to have a piece, but will stop himself. He'll give in eventually.*

Number one. This woman of yours – yes yours, not mine – is making my life a complete nightmare. Boys my age *aren't* tidy and clean and well behaved. We fart. It's totally...and they burp. It's normal. It's *not* normal to expect us to empty the bin in our bedroom every day. *Normal* boys shouldn't have to put all of their dirty clothes in the laundry basket. No other boy I know has to do the washing up after *every* meal. Number two. (NIGEL *takes a forkful of the pie and puts it in his mouth. He's at once livid and overtaken by how delicious the pie is) Shit* that's good. *(He'll have some more as he continues)* How is that so good? Two. Most of the boys I know are just allowed to be boys. Number three. Your neatly dressed, polite teenager, *(breaking)* has never felt so lonely in his entire life. I can do *nothing* right for this woman you've brought in to our lives. I hate her. And I hate you for loving her. Number four. It's never been OK, and it will never *be* OK, to give a fifteen-year-old slippers for their birthday.

DAD *(calling)* Nigel?

NIGEL *(regaining his composure as quickly as possible)* Dad?

DAD Here you are. I wanted to talk to you about something.

NIGEL What?

DAD The thing is, I've asked your Auntie Joan to marry me, and she's said yes.

NIGEL Wha—

DAD Isn't that good news? I think she's just like your mum, don't you?

NIGEL *is frozen.*

Come and celebrate with us? I've got some Walnut Whips and *The Persuaders* is just about to start.

Beat. **NIGEL** *gathers himself and joins* **DAD** *and* **JOAN** *in the sitting room.*

DAD Right then. Plain or coffee?

JOAN Oh plain please.

DAD Nigel? Are you joining us? Plain or coffee?

NIGEL Coffee for me please.

DAD Here we go then. Right, come on then, let's be having you Mr Moore.

DAD *opens the Walnut Whip, takes the walnut in his teeth, bites the top off, and licks into the cone.* **JOAN** *and* **NIGEL** *are opening their Whips as they realise what he's doing – they can't help staring at him.*

What?

JOAN What *are* you doing?

DAD Try it. Go on. *(He carries on, deeper and deeper into the cone)*

JOAN I will do no such thing you dirty—

NIGEL Dad! Stop it!

DAD Try it! Both of you! Nigel. Take the nut off the top, and then just bite the top off, see?

JOAN Tony!

DAD Right *(demonstrating as he's talking)* – and then you lick!

They are finding the situation funnier and funnier.

Come on. Deep in there! And the winner is the person who can get as much of the filling out as possible with just their tongue! There we go, look – *(showing an empty cone)* – that's how it's done.

NIGEL Sucking a flake isn't allowed, but apparently sticking your tongue as deep as you can into a Walnut Whip is. And so Friday evening becomes Walnut Whip Night. And now, a handful in my pockets, I'm walking up in the woods. I come here whenever I can, to get away for a bit. It's nearly nine o'clock, which is still my bedtime, even during the school holidays, but Joan and Dad will be too busy watching the television to come looking for me. At the lay-by just beyond the woods there's a row of cars facing the view, which goes all the way down the hill, and lights are starting to twinkle in the distance. People are sitting in the cars talking, some of them with their arms around – wait! There's one car over there with no one in it, so how is it – the car is swaying, violently back and forth. But there's no one there! I get a bit closer to have a look, and a bit closer still, and then – a pair of knees, wide apart, and someone's back, with no shirt on. A tiny bit closer and I'm nearly touching the side of the car. Suddenly I see the thing that's making the car sway – a bare, thrusting bottom. I must have stayed there for a few minutes – heart pounding, mouth so dry I have to lick out the filling of the Walnut Whip. After a couple more minutes the window opens and a hand pushes something wet out of the window, followed, before I can move, by a tissue. A split second later I'm on my feet, running, dropping the rest of the Whip as I go, all the way back home.

DAD Where have you been?

NIGEL *(taking off his jacket and putting it on a peg)* I just went out for a walk.

DAD You took three Walnut Whips with – what's *that* on the back of your jacket?

Beat.

NIGEL A little part of me dies that night – the little boy curled up on Dad's lap watching 'Dr Who' is gone in that moment, and there's no going back. And I can't stop. My trips to the lay-by soon become a nightly thing. A handful of Walnut Whips in hand, now wiped clean jacket on. I must be doing more walking than anyone else in the village put together. Fridays are still the busiest and best evenings, but closely followed by Saturdays.

DAD Hang on.

NIGEL What?

DAD Let me get my shoes on – I'm coming with you.

NIGEL The wedding is planned for two weeks' time, so that we're one big happy family for Christmas, and things haven't been good in recent weeks. Dad's coming for one of his 'try harder with Joan' chats.

DAD What's up with you, Nigel?

NIGEL Nothing.

DAD Joan does everything she can to make you happy. You mope around with a long face if she asks you to do anything, you don't speak to her unless she speaks to you first, you didn't even remember her birthday.

NIGEL She didn't remember mine.

DAD She's very fond of you. And you just throw it back in her face. She looks after you like her own son.

NIGEL I'm not her son.

DAD She's here, Nigel. And Mum's not. And if you don't like it you'll have to go in to care.

NIGEL Has getting rid of me *always* been an option to you?

DAD What?

NIGEL It doesn't matter. Everything's fine.

DAD Well make sure it is. I've had enough. OK?

> **NIGEL** *eventually nods.* **DAD** *hands him a Walnut Whip –
> a peace offering.*

> This is where the view is, just up here.

> *Beat. A moment of realisation.*

NIGEL Auntie Joan will be wondering where we are – why
don't we go home?

DAD She'll be fine. We've come all this way, we may as well.

NIGEL I can't think of a way to stop what seems to be just
about to happen. And then, before I can do anything, it *is*
happening. Half of Worcestershire is laid out before us. Acre
upon acre of fields rolling out for as far as you can see. But
that's not what Dad's looking at. He's looking down at the
tarmac of the lay by. To hundreds of used condoms. And
dozens of Walnut Whip wrappers. It's difficult to know at
that moment who wants to die most. We both do, of that
I'm certain.

> *We move to the wedding ceremony of* **DAD** *and* **JOAN** *–
> guests enter.*

> It's a small ceremony on a crisp, bright, sunny day, and both
> sides of the family are well represented, and, for a change,
> all surprisingly happy, and there are some of Joan's family
> I've never seen before—

JOAN Rose! This is my sister – Tony, Nigel.

ROSE Did you hear that?

DAD What?

ROSE There, again. *(Imitating the sound of birdsong)* Can you
not hear it?

JOAN Not to worry.

ROSE Where is it?

DAD Is she OK?

JOAN She has tinnitus – she can hear birds—

ROSE Sparrows—

JOAN – in her head. Oh, and there's Arnold.

ARNOLD Congratulations Joanie.

JOAN Tony, Nigel, this is my brother-in-law Arnold.

DAD Pleasure. Welcome.

ARNOLD Is it a free bar Joanie? Or—

JOAN It's not Arnold. Just the food.

ARNOLD Oh right, OK.

JOAN Haven't seen him in seven years. He'd turn up to the opening of a packet of fags if there was a free pint in it.

NIGEL There are more puddings than even Marguerite Pattern could name. And in the middle of everything, my wedding cake.

DAD *(taken aback, choked)* Oh my. Nigel.

> **DAD** *puts his arm around* **NIGEL**'s *shoulder as he admires the cake – three tiered, held up with white columns with diamond decorations, a bride and groom on the top and 'Tony & Joan' piped underneath.*

NIGEL It's Mum's Christmas cake recipe.

DAD How did you do the decorations?

NIGEL I got a book from the mobile library and saved up for the piping set.

DAD Joanie, would you look at this?

> **JOAN** *takes the cake in, inspects it.*

JOAN Hmm.

DAD I – Thank you.

NIGEL I bite my bottom lip to stop myself from crying, but suddenly Dad's grabbing me and hugging me.

DAD I didn't know a cake could look so beautiful. Thank you.

NIGEL As we drive the half an hour or so back to the house from the hotel, me in silence in the back of the car, I realise that I've never seen Dad looking happier.

A few days later – Christmas is in the air.

As traditional as Dad's Boxing Day turkey...fricassee—

DAD – Well done –

NIGEL – Thank you. And as traditional as his awful bay leaf joke, his sherry trifle is a pillar of the Slater Christmas experience. (**DAD** *picks up the spoon and goes to put it in to the trifle)* The noise when the spoon is lifted out is like a message from above. A silent trifle, like a silent jelly, is a bad omen. The louder the squelch-fart, the better things will be. But wait. We're getting ahead of ourselves. We need to make it first. And luckily Dad's already been at the sherry. So who better to tell us how to make the perfect trifle than Clayford's own Galloping Gourmet, Mr Tony Slater. Over to you Dad.

DAD Thank you. I would like to start by saying that I do use ready-made Swiss rolls, but I do *not* use custard powder, so. Nowadays everyone's using custard powder. It is absolutely unacceptable. Here are the Swiss rolls. They must be raspberry.

JOAN Not apricot?

DAD Not apricot, raspberry. And no interruptions thank you very much Mrs Slater. Now we put the sliced Swiss roll at the bottom of a glass bowl. With an apricot roll you just wouldn't be able to see the swirl properly. And pour over some peaches, a tin of peaches with the juice, and some sherry. It needs to soak in. Now jelly. Some people think a trifle should not include jelly. They are wrong.

NIGEL If Dad's trifle was a person, I'm pretty sure it would be a clown – one with stripey trousers and a red nose—

DAD We'll ignore that incredibly rude interjection and carry on with the – *(Beat)*—

JOAN Custard?

DAD Indeed, thank you. Custard. Not powder, as previously stated. Open the tin and pour that over the jelly. It is critical –

NIGEL – *Critical!* –

DAD – It is! It is vital that you do not let the custard run between the swiss roll slices and the glass. This will totally ruin the effect. Now we shall let is cool.

JOAN What are you going to put on top? Are we having hundreds and thousands?

DAD I shall pretend I didn't hear that Joan Slater – Mrs Potter. The last decade has not been kind to the trifle. It has had to contend with tinned apricots, hundreds and thousands, sliced bread instead of swiss roll, and, perhaps most humiliating of all, those awful, common teeth-shattering silver balls. The humble trifle used to grace our table as a favourite, only slightly tiddly aunt. Hundreds and thousands and the like have made her in to nothing more than an old tart in a leopardskin coat. Now. Cream. We cover it all with whipped cream –

JOAN – Here you go –

DAD – Thank you to my lovely assistant for fetching it. And then, on top of that, glacé cherries and whole almonds. And there we go. Sherry trifle.

NIGEL And now it's the moment of truth. Go for it Dad.

DAD *puts the spoon in to the trifle. It's silent.*

JOAN Did you hear anything?

DAD I didn't.

JOAN Nigel?

NIGEL Sorry.

DAD Well.

JOAN Well who ever thinks a trifle can decide how one day of the year is going to go needs their head examining. And that's all I have to say on the subject.

NIGEL The following day, it's the trifle that has the last word. Dad has decided to buy a hostess trolley so that we can have tea in the sitting room. It's a massive wooden thing, about six feet long, weighs a ton, and looks like the sort of thing you'd need an HGV licence to operate. Joan outdoes herself.

JOAN So we have ham with tomato water lilies –

NIGEL – Tomatoes that have been cut to look a bit like flowers –

JOAN And then salmon with wafer-thin cucumber in vinegar. And some sliced beetroot. And a veal and ham pie – it's got an egg in the middle. And some tongue –

NIGEL – That's for Dad –

JOAN – And then last but not least, a selection of (without the accent) crudites.

NIGEL – By which she means a plate of radishes and pickled onions.

DAD Oh Joan, how did you do it?

JOAN And then below on the second tier, to go with the the trifle, homemade mince pies and mandarin jelly for yourselves.

NIGEL The trolley has a magic toggle on it that allows the second tier to somehow rise up and join the top tier. But just as Dad's passing around the plates and I'm passing around parcels of napkins containing the cutlery, the toggle supporting the shelves pops out.

The entire trolley collapses – the food is thrown all over the place, covering the floor.

Only the trifle remains relatively unscathed. After Joan has cried and Dad has cleaned up, we try our best to put things back on track. We enthusiastically take a spoonful of trifle and do our best to enjoy it –

DAD It's lovely, honestly –

NIGEL – He winces, politely chewing the swiss roll, cream and pickled onion concoction he's put in his mouth.

Some time later.

NIGEL Maybe it's because I took last year's food war with Joan so seriously, but I start to realise that I am enjoying my cookery classes more and more, and with Michael and Tracey out of action for the holidays again, I decide to see if I can get a part-time job. Down the steepest hill in the world to the village and I'm at The Talbot – a huge, old, black and white pub on the edge of the river.

DOREEN How can I help?

NIGEL It's difficult to believe that this small woman, red hair and face full of freckles, is going to change everything. Sorry, I was just wondered if you had any – jobs? In the kitchen?

DOREEN As it happens we do need a bit of help on the weekends. How long have you been cooking? Where were you last?

NIGEL I'm not – I haven't. I don't – I want to learn.

DOREEN Round the back, glass door. We'll give you a go.

NIGEL Thank you! I go around to the back of the hotel and knock on the glass door, and—

DOREEN – Come in then.

NIGEL Sorry – how many people work in the kitchen then?

DOREEN It's me. Me in the kitchen. Me on the bar. Me. That OK with you?

NIGEL Yes, sorry. I was just wondering.

DOREEN Wonder less. Get an apron, I'll show you around.

> **NIGEL** *puts on an apron while* **DOREEN** *shows him around the kitchen.*
>
> It's small, but we get a lot done. Work station in the middle is for the veg, and then over there, pot wash, stoves here, knives there if you don't have your own, up at the back the fridges. And then up here the store – mixing bowls, pie dishes, tart tins, spices, measuring scales, cheese cutter, anything you need.

NIGEL It's incredible.

DOREEN It's better. Incredible's a way off. I took over a year ago. The place used to be full of freezers. Main courses in plastic pouches with labels – boeuf bourguignon, coq au vin, veal cordon bleu, duck a l'orange –

NIGEL – Duck a l'orange? Peel two oranges and cut the peel into very narrow ribbons. Simmer in a little water –

DOREEN – Where did you get that from?

NIGEL I read a lot of cookbooks. Or rather, I read a cookbook a lot.

DOREEN Right. Be careful of recipes. I'm not interested in someone else's taste. OK? I want *your* taste.

NIGEL *(remembering, smiling) Our* tarts.

DOREEN What?

NIGEL Nothing. I –

DOREEN – The level of food under the last owners was defrosting paté and prawns and chopping up lettuce. That's not what I want to do. I buy from local shops, markets, the butcher, fishmonger, delicatessen, cheese shops. Tonight we've got pork and game pie – we got some lovely rabbit and pigeon in this morning.

NIGEL I like Doreen almost immediately. That night I go home having sliced runner beans, made a cheese sauce, and filleted a rabbit.

JOAN I hope she paid you?

NIGEL She hadn't, but said she would at the end of the week if I did a good enough job. To be honest I don't care if she never pays me – I have never enjoyed myself so much in my life.

JOAN Go and have a bath, you stink.

NIGEL I go upstairs to my room, hot, sticky and bursting with excitement. Bugger Joan. I'm a chef now.

DOREEN Right, we've got rolled rib of beef, chicken or lamb today. Do you want to look after the veg and Yorkshires?

NIGEL It's Sunday lunch at The Talbot. Doreen teaches me to make the highest, most cloud-like Yorkshire puddings I've ever seen. Roast potatoes that are golden and crunchy on the outside but melty and soft in the middle. Gravy that shines—

DOREEN Taste, taste, taste. What does it need?

NIGEL I—

DOREEN Salt. Never hold back on salt. It brings food to life.

NIGEL I'm learning more over the weekend than Miss Adams managed to teach in a whole year of domestic science lessons, and I'm loving every moment.

DOREEN How old are you, then, if you don't mind me asking.

NIGEL Sixteen. Going on seventeen. Like the film. How old are you?

DOREEN You can clean out the fryer for that you cheeky bugger. My son's seventeen.

NIGEL Where is he?

DOREEN Royal Ballet School in London. He'll be back for the summer holidays though.

NIGEL I can't imagine it's easy having a ballet dancer for a son. 'One of them' as Joan says. 'Nancy boys' as Dad says. But I don't say anything. How long have you been cooking?

DOREEN Not long – Ken and I ran a farm before this. Plumridge Farm, about an hour away.

NIGEL What made you change?

DOREEN Cooking, if you get it right, is creative. It's gratifying. It's one of the greatest pleasures you can have with your clothes on.

NIGEL Up until this point it would be fair to say that excepting Walnut Whips, most of the pleasure I've had in life has been clothed. As the summer gets hotter, it seems like that may be about to change.

DOREEN I think someone fancies you.

NIGEL Who?

DOREEN Girl out the front who's been throwing stares this way all evening. Go on, go and see her. Say hello.

NIGEL I can't, how about the—

DOREEN Go – I can cover any orders than come in.

NIGEL The girl is Julia. Violet eyes, dark hair, she sits for hours in the front while her parents drink, pretending to read but actually staring over – at me, or rather, as I discover, at the tray of drinks on the bar that builds up each night from mistaken orders. And so it happens that whenever it's slow in the kitchen, I've started taking her a tray drink. One night she suggests a walk down by the river. We walk side by side, not speaking much, until we come to an oak tree next to the river whose roots have come up above the ground like some sort of wooden tangle of snakes. We sit there for what feels like forever. Suddenly her top's off and she's telling me to hurry up, she's got to get back. In the lay by I had seen enough people shagging to last me a lifetime. But now, here, I can't remember anything.

DOREEN So? How's your girlfriend?

NIGEL She's not – it's a few weeks later and I'm making a prawn and salmon mousse for a new plaice dish Doreen's adding tonight – she's not my girlfriend.

DOREEN Suit yourself.

NIGEL *(to the audience)* It's true, she's not my girlfriend. The tray drinks-for-sex deal works for both of us, but that's all it is. Neat, tidy and predictable.

STUART enters. He seems at first incredibly confident, especially when in DOREEN's company, but on his own he is a lot more tentative, even shy.

And then – who's *that*?

DOREEN That's Stuart! Stuart!

STUART Mum!

DOREEN How are you? I didn't know you were arriving this evening.

STUART Surprise. *(To NIGEL)* Hi. I'm Stuart.

NIGEL Hi. I'm Stuart.

STUART That's me—

NIGEL Sorry, Nigel. I'm Nigel. Hi.

DOREEN I'll have to make your bedroom up darling. If you'd have told me I could have made some Malvern pud to celebrate. Tomorrow, I'll make it tomorrow.

NIGEL Stuart. Stuart the ballet dancer. Tall. Confident. Good-look—

STUART – Who are you talking to?

DOREEN – He does this a lot—

NIGEL – I wasn't, I. *(Pause)* Doreen, your mum –

DOREEN – He knows who I am.

NIGEL Sorry, I just mean't – your mum said you're at the Royal Ballet School in London?

STUART Second year, my dear.

NIGEL What's it like? Do you mind me asking?

STUART Endless. Solos. Rep. Pas de deux. And that's just classical. Then there's contemporary, Irish, Morris, pretty much everything else under the sun. Body conditioning *every* morning.

NIGEL I meant, sorry I meant London.

STUART *(to* **DOREEN***)* Does he mean to say he's never been?

NIGEL I'd like to. I'm going to. It's just – have you been to the food hall at Fortnum and Mason? Or Chinatown?

STUART Oh Mum we *have* to get young Nigel up to the bright lights.

DOREEN Oh he'd love it. Right, I'll take your things up. *(Leaving with* **STUART***'s bags, hugging and kissing him as she goes)* Darling!

They are left alone together. **STUART***'s confidence has disappeared.*

NIGEL Tell me about Chinatown?

STUART We're cooped up down in Baron's Court, we don't really get to go out much. What about you? You're...from around here?

NIGEL Just up the hill.

STUART Is Julia still around trying to shag everything that moves?

NIGEL Err –

STUART I take it you've met then.

NIGEL I – we're not. I'm—

Pause.

STUART You're—

NIGEL I don't—

DOREEN *enters, breaking the moment.*

DOREEN Right. Now, shall we get ready for service Nigel? What are you going to do, darling?

STUART I've been in a car for hours. I need some fresh air. Why don't you come with me Nigel? Show me the way – I haven't been back in months, I don't want to get lost. If that's alright Mum?

DOREEN Course. Go on then. I can manage here.

NIGEL Are you sure?

DOREEN I wouldn't say it if I didn't mean it.

NIGEL It's an awkward walk. Just as awkward as my walk only a few weeks before with Julia. Long silences, neither of us apparently knowing what to say. *(Silence)* Hang on, I've got to pee.

NIGEL *leaves* STUART *– he finds a spot, unzips his fly. As he's relieving himself* STUART *comes down to him, slides his arms around* NIGEL's *neck, and pulls his face slowly towards him.*

STUART Hi.

NIGEL Hi.

They kiss, and then break away.

And that's it. We run back to the hotel, and—

STUART – See you later –

NIGEL As he bounces up to his room, I go back to the kitchen. Butterflies in my stomach but at the same time a bit... disappointed. I thought being 'one of them' was going to be more exciting.

DOREEN *(entering)* Nigel. Would you come out front?

NIGEL Of course. Has Stuart said something already? Whatever it is, it's not good. I follow her out to the bar, and—

JOAN *appears in front of him.*

JOAN Nigel. I've got something to tell you. Your dad was playing tennis this afternoon, and...

She breaks down. Pause. NIGEL *isn't sure what to do.* DOREEN *pushes him towards* JOAN, *who he goes to reluctantly. She hugs him tightly.*

DOREEN *(to* JOAN*)* Come on. Have a seat and let's get something strong down you. Nigel love – you go and get your things and take your mum home.

NIGEL She's – *(Beat)* I go back in to the kitchen. I feel like I should be crying. But I can't. I bite my bottom lip hard – not to stop the tears, but to check that this is really happening.

For a few moments NIGEL *is at a loss. He moves things, stands still, paces, tries to make sense of what is happening. After a while he sees a tray of mushrooms. A moment of realisation. From here on in he is in a world of his own. Things will come together slowly at first, and then faster, as he is taken over by an increasingly urgent need to cook. He clears the various things away from his bench. He chops the mushrooms and wild garlic, dices an onion, takes some butter and thyme and adds everything to a frying pan. He slices a piece of bread and grills it. The whole process will take a few minutes but the audience should be there with* NIGEL, *as everything starts to come together, as the atmosphere intensifies, as he plates up the toast and gently topples the pan-fried mushrooms on it, topping the mushrooms with some crumbled blue cheese. As he's finishing it,* DOREEN *comes back in to the kitchen –.*

DOREEN Nigel—

NIGEL *can't speak. He simply stands with his plate of food. After a couple of moments* DOREEN *goes over to him, taking a fork, and tries the food.*

Recipe?

NIGEL *shakes his head.*

Nigel, this is – now go on. You need to look after her.

He gathers his things. Makes to leave.

And Nigel?

He turns.

This is going on the lunch menu, OK?

NIGEL *smiles, and leaves. A few days later.*

As funerals go – and I'm starting to think I know what I'm talking about – Dad's is beautiful. There are flowers everywhere – as you'd hope for a man who put gardening right up there on a par with sex. The weather held out, and the vicar was as respectful as could be expected for having only just having met my Dad, boxed, a day ago. There's something about a group of people in church, singing 'Lord of all Hopefulness', a small organ accompanying – *(Losing his composure)*. Joan makes a big deal of fussing over me – I don't know if she cares, whether it's her way of coping, or whether she's worried about the will. It doesn't matter. Because I'm free. Without Mum, without Dad, there's nothing keeping me here, in this house, with this woman who had done *nothing* but make my life a misery. I'm seventeen. I can do whatever I want. And I know exactly what that is. I want to cook.

We are taken to Worcester Catering College – enter MICHAEL *and* TRACEY *as well as the* LECTURER, *preparing for class.*

(shocked to see his school friends again) What are *you* doing here? Mike?

MICHAEL What, we can't come to catering college too? You need a bit of competition, Slater. And I can't muck out stables all my life.

NIGEL Trace?

TRACEY Yes?

NIGEL What about you? I didn't have you down as a chef.

TRACEY I don't know.

LECTURER Settle down everyone. *(Holding up a copy of Larousse Gastronomique)* Cookery's version of the King James, yes? So – Escoffier's Mother Sauces. Anyone? You.

MICHAEL Béchamel. Espagnole. Tomate. Umm hollandaise. And...velouté.

LECTURER Correct. Espagnole – you – go.

NIGEL One carrot. One onion. One celery. One butter. One flour. Four beef or veal stock. Quarter purée tomato. Bay leaf. S and P to season.

LECTURER Precisely. Béchamel? – Yes? –

TRACEY *(looking blank – tentatively)* Besher?

LECTURER Never mind. How about *(flicking through the book)* – who can tell me how to make a Mornay?

Hands go up in the classroom.

Yes – you.

MICHAEL Mornay sauce – three butter, three flour, three milk, two Gruyère, two—

LECTURER Why Gruyère?

MICHAEL Sir?

LECTURER You said Gruyère. Why? Why not Comté? Or bring it closer to home – why not a good old cheddar?

MICHAEL I—

LECTURER You need to get past ratting off lists of ingredients. *Lists* of ingredients are just rules. Break the fucking rules. Cook by *taste*. If something tastes good, it's right. No one gets to tell you what goes with what. Some flavours work together – think tomato and basil. Try it. Think about *why* it works. Yes, it's helpful to have the basics, to understand Escoffier, Carême, but don't be a bloody slave. In London right now, what do you think they're doing? Poncing around with their Larousse reeling off Mornay? Course they're fucking not. They're exploring. They're breaking the rules. Parma ham. Melon. It shouldn't work should it? But think about that salt in the ham intensifying the flavour of the melon. Chicken with tarragon. Fennel and blood orange. Work it out. Work out what works for *you*. And when you finish here, you'll have a choice. Stay around here with your little recipe bibles, or get to London, Paris, Lyon, Naples, Rome, and *cook*.

NIGEL Finishing at college comes around faster than any of us think it will, but not before my birthday.

MICHAEL and TRACEY enter with a cake, presents and bottles of wine, singing ***"HAPPY BIRTHDAY"****. A radio plays in the background – towards the end of the scene Julio Iglesias's cover of* ***"LA MER"*** *will start to play. They settle down, pouring drinks and cutting cake.*

MICHAEL Right then. A toast. To Nigel, who is eighteen and who we love.

BOTH To Nigel.

NIGEL And to the future.

ALL To us. And to the future.

MICHAEL So? Plans? Tracey, what are you going to do?

TRACEY The Sun Hotel.

NIGEL Where's that?

TRACEY I don't know. It smells a bit of hoover bag but it's got net curtains and Russian salad.

MICHAEL What's in Russian salad?

TRACEY Whatever we can find that's Russian. Carrots. Potatoes. Peas?

MICHAEL None of that's Russian.

NIGEL *(to* MICHAEL*)* How about you?

MICHAEL The Fountain. In Bromsgrove. It's disgusting. The fridges are opposite the loos and next to the bins, and there were dead cockroaches everywhere on the floor. On my trial shift I had to do the fish and chips.

NIGEL And?

MICHAEL Doing the fish meant washing last night's batter off the fish and re-covering it. Chef says it's the batter that goes off, not the fish.

TRACEY I've heard that.

NIGEL Hopefully you don't have to stay there too long?

MICHAEL No way. I want The Markham House Hotel with my brother. In Worcester?

NIGEL That's supposed to be nice. Two restaurants?

MICHAEL Aphrodite's and the hotel restaurant. It's all black forest gateau and chicken Kiev and prawn cocktail and vegetables of the day in the hotel restaurant, but in Aphrodite's its French. Steak Diane, shallots and brandy and apparently everyone's having sex with everyone else. What about you?

NIGEL Joan's moving back to Wolverhampton. She called to ask if I'd like to move in with her. Get a job around there.

MICHAEL And?

NIGEL *listens to* **"LA MER"** – *silence.*

NIGEL I learned to dance to this song.

Beat.

TRACEY Can I ask you a question Nigel?

MICHAEL Bloody hell! It only took four years to get his name right.

TRACEY Is she asking for you? Or for her?

Beat. We are transported to London.

NIGEL I arrive in London early on a Tuesday morning in December, frozen, with a backpack and with just enough money for a couple of rounds of toast and a coffee in a greasy looking café. There are shops everywhere, and even more people. Theatres, restaurants, a train and underground station one end and a huge church in the middle of the road at the other. I turn a corner to a shimmering silver canopy, the world's flags and a blazing statue on top. Five emerald letters. Savoy. And just around from the main entrance, the service alley.

We find SAVOY CHEF, in 'Savoy Grill' whites, standing and smoking.

SAVOY CHEF What are you after?

NIGEL Sorry. I don't suppose—

SAVOY CHEF That was my last one mate.

NIGEL No, sorry. I was just wondering if you have any jobs going? In the kitchen?

SAVOY CHEF You're a chef?

NIGEL I can cook.

SAVOY CHEF Whites and knives?

NIGEL I – no, I don't.

SAVOY CHEF Pastry, larder, meat, fish or garnish?

NIGEL I—

SAVOY CHEF Well?

NIGEL I think I can – probably pastry?

SAVOY CHEF Probably? It's barely three weeks to Christmas – we've got over two hundred individual Christmas cakes and nearly eight thousand mince pies to make from scratch, we haven't got time for—

NIGEL I can make mince pies.

SAVOY CHEF Recipe?

NIGEL I'd need to scale it.

SAVOY CHEF I haven't got all day.

NIGEL It's—

> **NIGEL** *is remembering back to making mince pies with* **MUM** *– she is with him.*

MUM Get the rolling pin out then, let's get them done. Can you remember what we need?

NIGEL It's ten ounces of flour. Four butter. And one ounce lard.

SAVOY CHEF Go on.

NIGEL Ummm... *(Struggling)*

MUM Sugar?

NIGEL Two! Two teaspoons of caster sugar—

MUM Tick.

NIGEL One egg yolk.

MUM Tick. And last but not least?

NIGEL A pound of mincemeat – more or less.

> *Blackout.*

PROPS LIST

3 x lightweight but sturdy 1960's dining chairs
1 x green wing back chair with chintz loose cover (wheels on back legs)
1 x practical period standard lamp
Full stainless steel kitchen cabinets, benches, cooker, sink etc..

ACT ONE

Cookery in Colour by Marguerite Patten
Mixing bowl, flour, baking tray, tea towel
Bowl of dough
Tray of jam tarts
Jam/Curd/Marmalade jars - will need usable jam/curd per performance
Plates
Two metal wheelbarrows with compost, spade and seeds
Metal pans and lids (approx. 20) flown
Coffee percolator (practical)
Cups and saucers (1960's)
Tin of shortbread petticoats
3 x period suitcases
Circular table with double sided cloth (peach/red) lightweight
Floral table display (can have the flowers in the water jug)
Menu's glasses, water jug, candlestick
Wheelbarrow as before with radishes planted
Towel
Top of the form name labels attached to counters
Large shiny plate of biscuits
Three plates of food, ham lettuce and tomato
8 flown lampshades
Hot Ribena in glass with handle (corning snap)
Steaming bowl of porridge with spoon
Preset in top cupboards the following period packaging
    1. Turkish delight in wooden boxes
    2. Crystallised Figs
    3. Sugared plums
    4. Jars of cherries soaked in brandy
    5. Currants
    6. Carton of icing sugar

7. Bottles of Mateus
Brown paper grocery bag
Scales, mixing bowl, wooden spoon
Unseen tray of flour in cabinet
Fruit cake
Marzipan covered cake
Flat iced cake
Peaked iced cake with snowman and tree

ACT TWO

Rolling pin
Pre rolled pastry
Mince pie tin
Cutter

2 pink marshmallows
round table as before
      Flower decoration
      Trick white table cloth see: https://www.youtube.com/
watch?v=nSj_MVUsBzg
      Sundae dish with long spoon
Plastic dessert bowl and spoon
7 x flown oversize sweet jars with wings
Plates with – boiled egg, poached egg, fried egg and scrambled
egg
Frying pan with sausage and bacon
Packing boxes x8
Kitsch vase
Apple pie
Three small bowls and spoons
Cake tin
Victoria sponge on cake stand
Sieve with icing sugar
2 x hostess trolleys with food stuff to throw
Lemon meringue pie
3 x walnut whips (period packaging, plain,vanilla and coffee)
Cellophane walnut whip wrappers (many)
Rectangular white cloth to cover table
Three tier columned wedding cake
Trifle lecture cards A2

Traditional trifle in see through bowl with spoon
Central selection of flown pans from Act 1
Chopping board and knife
Bowl and whisk
Cooking (tbc)

LIGHTING

Lights up p1
Lights down p41
Spotlight on Christmas cake p42
Lights up on Nigel p42
Blackout p86

SOUND EFFECTS

A hive of industry, or chaos p13
Knock at the door p25
Doorbell rings p25
Charles Trenet's *La Mer* plays p31
It is winter – air of festivity floods the stage p34
Bell rings for lunchtime p58
A bell goes p60
A radio plays in the background p83
Julio Iglesia's *La Mer* plays p83
London p85
Savoy Grill kitchen sounds p85

THIS
IS
NOT
THE
END

Lightning Source UK Ltd.
Milton Keynes UK
UKHW020515080219
336901UK00005B/635/P